PRISONER NO MORE

The Ultimate Guide for Achieving Freedom,
Lasting Change, and True Potential

DANTE B. KUN

Copyright © 2022 Dante B. Kun

All rights reserved. No part of this publication in print or in electronic format may be reproduced, stored in a retrieval system, or transmitted in any form or by any means, electronic, mechanical, photocopying, recording, or otherwise without the prior written permission of the publisher.

The scanning, uploading, and distribution of this book without permission is a theft of the author's intellectual property. Thank you for your support of the author's rights.

This book is not intended as a substitute for the medical advice of physicians or psychiatrists. The reader should regularly consult a physician in matters relating to his/her health and particularly with respect to any symptoms that may require diagnosis or medical/psychiatric attention. Although the author and publisher have made every effort to ensure that the information in this book was correct at press time, the author and publisher do not assume and hereby disclaim any liability to any party for any loss, damage, or disruption caused by errors or omissions, whether such errors or omissions result from negligence, accident, or any other cause.

Design and distribution by Bublish, Inc.

ISBN: 978-1-647044-68-8 (eBook)
ISBN: 978-1-647044-76-3 (paperback)

Dedicated to the quest for true freedom within all people everywhere.

INTRODUCTION

This is a book about personal, spiritual, financial, and relational survival. It is a book about reclaiming your life from dysfunction and pain. This book was born in the darkness of Pelican Bay State Prison, where I worked as a Case Management Specialist for fifteen years. For the last seven years, I have been a Directing Clinician and Clinical Supervisor at an addiction treatment facility. Make no mistake, this is not "just a book" for inmates or addicts. This is a book for family members as well as anyone facing turmoil and challenge because it addresses the difficulties all humans face in creating, sustaining, and thriving in life. This is a book for survivors. While at Pelican Bay, I had an epiphany: prisons are just microcosms of society at large. This realization came about when I found out that staff, inmate families, friends, and community volunteers were using the exercises within this manual. Though interpersonal challenges may differ in some ways they are also similar as well. Trauma comes to all in many forms. We are all serving a life sentence on the third rock from the sun. We are spiritual beings having physical experiences. Some people are behind physical bars within physical prisons, and some are trapped inside invisible prisons. They are all doing "time." These visible and invisible chains drain our life, moment by precious moment. If we allow them, they will direct our path in life. They will eventually stop us from progressing altogether.

I soon learned that the difference between "inmate" and "free people" is not as great as we imagine it to be. Someday, physical experiences will end for all people. We learn lessons during physical life and the lessons will continue until learned. This is the nature of being a spiritual being in a physical body.

In chapter three 3 we will address regret, anger, and guilt. These are three heavy chains, and they are devastating to those suffering their burden. Consider this from chapter three: The only action you can take in the present moment is to accept the past and its lessons, learn from those lessons, and move on. Any other action allows the past to rule your present moment, and all you have is your present moment. Regret is a time bandit. Don't allow regret to rob you of your present moment in time.

This workbook was originally made for people on parole or probation and their loved ones. Although prison has special challenges to overcome, we all have challenges that overlap. I invite you to do the exercises within and feel the positive results. This workbook will help you learn how to choose what you love to do, regardless of the opinions of others. You will be encouraged to listen to the whisperings of your heart. The past is dead; you are not your past. The future has not yet happened. You have only the present moment, moment to moment. Your choices within each moment will become your future. Seeing this process can begin growth in a new direction. This is true regardless of your present circumstances. Inmate or free, we all have a "life sentence." How we manage that is entirely up to us.

This book is a journey into the world within you. As such, it will guide you on a journey into your unknown self. It will also guide you back and you may find that in the process your old way of life will have become invalidated by new growth. A true miracle happens when you find your inner strength and use it to heal and grow a new life with renewed purpose.

In chapter four, we will go on a journey back in time. We will cover millions of years in an instant. You will learn beyond a shadow of doubt that you are a true and present miracle. "The Tale of the Earthtribe" has led many people out of the two-camp continuum of "them" and "us." Take the journey and see for yourself. Learn how to leave racism and bigotry in the rear-view mirror. Learn to embrace the magic of humanity.

Don't allow fear-based, defensive thinking to crush authentic communication and healthy dialogue. Defensive/divisive thinking is a prison skill. Open-minded thinking is a free-world skill. The free world is filled with people from all over the planet. In prison, you were manipulated to only associate with "your kind." You can do that in the free world, but you are missing out on new experiences. I'm not saying to just blindly trust everyone, use reasonable caution. I am saying that it is not wise to write everyone off and be an island unto yourself. Humans are social, so get social. Learning about different ideas, lifestyles, cultures, and customs will develop your social perspective. This is a good thing, and it only makes you stronger. It can sometimes be a struggle, but being open to other people's ideas and views on politics, culture, customs, and social morals, will only increase your empathic abilities. Learning to respect others' views and gaining cultural empathy can only make you a better communicator and a better person.

If you have tried other self-help books with limited results, I invite you to try this one. The exercises inside have helped transform lives within one of the most violent prisons in America. Trust the process and try something few "free people" have ever tried. Step into a prisoner's shoes for a short time. You may walk away a different person, a better person, a stronger person. If you have a loved one or a friend on parole or supervision, this workbook will help you understand their challenges as well as some of your own.

If you are on parole or probation, you are in a system designed to record and document (correctly and sometimes incorrectly) your worst decisions. Time is irrelevant to this system because they want all your time. The system is self-sustaining, and it will never stop monitoring you. No matter how many degrees you earn, no matter your attainment of ongoing success or stability, no matter how successful your "rehabilitation" turns out, the system has you marked for life. This is a survival manual, and its success in your life depends upon your ability to start becoming a social being within the twenty-first century. My goal is to foster and share an open exchange of information, resources, and guidelines. The content has been shaped by my day-to-day interaction with inmates, parolees, and probationers from the California State Prison system, the Alaska State Prison system, county jails, and the Federal Prison system. For almost three decades I have worked with thousands of inmates and parole violators, who either returned to the system or were on parole or probation and were attempting to finally exit the system. My focus has been to find tough answers to questions of survival that are usually ignored and seldom asked or focused upon.

The recidivism rate for adult offenders within California has been as high as eighty-seven percent in some years. No matter what state you choose to examine, it seems that prison and jail are just systems with revolving doors. Most adult offenders seem hopelessly trapped within a grim and ever circular ritual of offense, incarceration, probation/parole, rearrest, reincarceration, and probation/parole yet again. They are doing life within prison walls as well as outside prison and jail on an expensive installment plan. Expensive to the taxpayers fiscally. Tragically expensive to prisoners and their families emotionally, psychologically, and sometimes even physically.

This almost constant and guaranteed recidivism is a reality often commented on and conversed about within correctional and rehabilitation circles. No one seems to have a definitive answer regarding a viable solution to this harsh reality. The major tactic so far is to talk about recidivism and then promptly ignore some of its obvious causes: A permanent, sustainable wage employment ban, a permanent lockout from key professions, denial of housing, education, and co-occurring societal alienation,(just to name a few.) As a society, we need more than just strong opinions. We need to exert our critical faculties and admit that perhaps we need to look at things differently. The taxpayers will ultimately thank us in the long run.

This situation is grim but not hopeless. Within this workbook, you will find important survival questions, not only about parole, probation, and supervision but also about life itself and one's personal relationship to life. This workbook will examine how one approaches life, what judgments about life we hold, and what expectations we hold.

Also, the reader will be challenged to examine how well these thought constructs serve the higher good of society as well as themselves. Ultimately you will become your own solution because the system is generally not willing or able to help you. It is up to you to survive parole, and it will be up to you to attain and sustain your freedom. This book can help you with those goals.

Current prerelease programs are simply not working very well. At tens of thousands of dollars per inmate per year, society must go in new directions regarding prerelease training programs. If inmates cannot be transformed into productive citizens and taxpayers, then prison and parole systems are failures. They have simply become giant holes into which society pours money. As a society, we cannot continue the old ways of doing things without making the taxpayers suffer.

Using the California State Prison system as an example, taxpayers are spending over a billion dollars a year to keep roughly 180,000 people incarcerated. (Although there are movements afoot to reduce this number in California, I hold very little optimism for meaningful change.) That is 180,000 people out of a population of about thirty-four million. If this were graphed out mathematically, the people incarcerated in state prisons would not even be a full percentage point of the overall population. Think about that for a moment. The budget of a third-world country is spent and essentially thrown away each year, all to keep a piece of a percentage point of the population locked up. I am not even factoring in the costs of county jails and federal facilities. The humble suggestions within the following pages constitute a workbook, not only about parole survival but about the social world we all must ultimately survive and hopefully thrive within.

How to Use This Book

I will review key concepts along the way. This might seem repetitive. That is OK with me because there are important things you need to understand. I will remind you of them from time to time. You might even thank me later. At the end of each chapter, there will be exercises and some personal development questions to answer. To get the most benefit out of the workbook, please write out the questions in a separate journal or notebook and then write out your answers. Writing out your answers as well as the questions will slow your mind down a bit and work your brain somewhat differently than speaking. You can then go back over your notebook and reexamine the questions and your observations over time. You may notice that some of your answers will change as time goes on. Change is a good thing; don't resist change. Your old way of life will eventually become invalidated by new growth. Change is unstoppable. Change is an unstoppable dynamic of the multiverse and it cannot be denied. People, places, and things will change, and failing to accept change will not serve your higher good.

Personal Development Questions

The exercises in this workbook are here to help you gain social, emotional, spiritual, and interpersonal skills. They are here to help you develop your emotional intelligence. Ultimately, they are here to challenge you and to help you learn the lessons of your heart. They will help you know yourself better. Some of these questions may be painful for you. Work through the pain. Sometimes new growth can be a bit uncomfortable. The purpose of each question is to help you grow in new directions. If you are in prison, jail, or on probation or parole, the universe has put you on notice. You simply cannot continue the old way and not suffer. You cannot continue the old way and not have your family suffer along with you. Your old way of life has been invalidated by a demand for new growth and the universe is demanding this new growth immediately. I suggest you listen.

Learning about yourself and healing your past is one of the greatest things you can do to better yourself. Healing yourself and growing in new directions can become a catalyst for healing your relationships with your family and society. Self-healing will lead you away from incarceration. Losing your freedom is almost always the result and predictable outcome of a dysfunctional interpersonal relationship between yourself and someone else. It is also an obvious conflict between yourself and your society or culture. Growth is not always a comfortable process. True growth takes effort and commitment. Right now—THIS MINUTE—you have the opportunity to better yourself. I wish you luck on this new journey.

Affirmations

At the end of each chapter is an affirmation. I recommend that you speak your affirmation within your mind each night as you drift off to sleep. I also think you should say your affirmation to yourself for a few moments as you are waking up and preparing for your day. As you go through your day, bring your focus internally to your affirmation from time to time. If you experience negative thoughts, overwhelm them with your affirmations. As you go through the chapters, use the affirmations daily, and feel free to mix them up throughout the week. However, I recommend that you focus on only one each day.

If you have engaged in a lot of negative thinking, you cannot expect to use an affirmation for only a minute or two each day and expect a quick result. Every negative and self-limiting thought you use is an affirmation all on its own. For your affirmations to be successful, you must be willing to use them every day and use them a lot! Affirmations can really help you notice self-limiting thoughts and beliefs because you will use them each time a negative thought comes up. Your awareness of your own internal dialogue will be raised. You will begin replacing negative thoughts with positive, life-affirming thoughts. This will take some work on your part, but it will become enjoyable work eventually.

Remember, your chosen affirmation should be the last thing you say to yourself as you are falling asleep, and the first thought on your mind when you wake up each morning.

Allowing your ego to rule your choices leads only to despair. Everyone else will be wrong, and you will always be right. You will win every battle and lose the ultimate war for your freedom. Even when you are free of the criminal justice system, you will be an inmate. You will think like an inmate and act like an inmate. You will eventually return to the place where inmates live out their lives. A world of steel cages, cement, and championship-level sociopaths. All of it will reflect your choices.

You cannot change the past or how your past choices and decisions have affected you and those you love. There is only one healthy path open to you right now in this present moment: change the way you live in the present by making healthy new choices. All your healthy choices right now are creating a positive future that is yet unknown to you. Society has removed its chunk of flesh, Lady Justice has balanced the scales, and the judge has banged the gavel. It's time to move on. You have survived prison—now survive parole. Choose to thrive and not just survive.

The sociopath's motto is: "Laws don't apply to me."

The sociopath's slogan is: "I didn't do it." (Evidence does not matter.)

The sociopath's oath is: "If I did it, I have a good reason and you should leave me alone about it."

I am not calling you a sociopath. I am just pointing out observable perceptions. At some point in time, you learned to look out for yourself at the expense of others. You may have become excellent at denying all responsibility for your choices or decisions. You may have learned to manipulate others. You may have accepted "freedom from choice." The culture of criminality is a lot like the culture of addiction. Everyone is out for themselves. Relationships are just tools for accomplishing dysfunctional "goals." People, places, and things can put your freedom at risk in the same way they can put sobriety at risk.

CONTENTS

Chapter 1	Life on the Installment Plan	1
Chapter 2	Choices	13
Chapter 3	Guilt, Anger, Regret	27
Chapter 4	The Tale of the Earthtribe	43
Chapter 5	Presenting Yourself to the World	67
Chapter 6	Becoming Employed	85
Chapter 7	Look Truthfully at Your Life	105
Chapter 8	Recommended Reading List and Resources	113

CHAPTER ONE

Life on the Installment Plan

"Challenges create life."
—Dante B. Kun

The current situation in the United States is challenging for anyone on parole or probation. Almost every state has a three-strikes law or habitual criminal legislation. Getting rearrested and convicted becomes a gift that keeps on giving. The more you re-offend, the more time you face until you are doing time measured in double digits. It is quite possible for a judge to be painted into a corner due to these presumptive and accumulative sentencing laws. Even if they are sympathetic to your case and feel that justice is not served regarding the harshness of the sentence, a state legislature may have essentially made the decision for them. Their hands may be tied. The imposition and length of sentence may be a state-legislated calculation. You can keep on earning violations, enhancements, and extended sentences on an unhealthy continuum. Then one day you wake up and realize that you have been in prison for more time than you have been free.

I work with people who are struggling with drug addiction. Many of them are in survival situations. I think that being on parole or probation qualifies as a survival situation. I often ask my clients to look up the meaning of the word "survival." I want you to be clear about your tactical situation. I want you to know the actual meaning of the word, not your assumption of the word. Meanings are important. I would like you to consider the meaning of the word "survival." *Webster's New World Dictionary, Third College Edition*, defines survival as: "the act, state, or fact of surviving." It goes on to define survival as: "something or someone who survives." Researching a bit further in Webster's, we find the word "survive." The definition of surviving I like best is: "to continue to live after or in spite of." The example used in Webster's is: "to continue to live after, or in spite of, a shipwreck." If you are in prison, in jail, or on parole, your life is officially a "shipwreck." You are not sailing through life; you are crashing upon the rocks of the criminal justice system. No ship ever created can sail upon rocks and remain afloat.

As an ex-felon and a probationer/parolee, you have some tough challenges ahead of you. The first challenge is realizing that there is no such thing as an "ex-felon" in the United States. Once a felon, always a felon in the good old USA. Becoming a felon is a life sentence. Almost no one cares about the harsh reality of being a felon or its impact on employment and day-to-day life. You will be challenged to survive and thrive despite your felony convictions, despite the toughest laws society has devised thus far to lock you up FOREVER. Make no mistake about this fact: habitual criminal laws, three-strikes laws, and enhancements all came about by legislation designed to lock up the continual "problem children" and throw away the key. In some very crucial and important ways, society will neither forget your past nor let you forget it. This is because society fears criminals. Do not resent society for the fear-based thinking that pervades crime and punishment issues. It may not be fair, but sometimes it is well-founded.

I am going to ask you to use your powers of imagination for a minute. Imagine that you were working a stressful job of forty to sixty hours a week. You are a single parent balancing daycare for two children, a car payment, rent, food, and clothing, and you are the sole support for your two children, ages three and five. You love them more than life itself. Imagine that you come home one day after picking up your children from daycare. Your house has been broken into and your TV, laptop, stereo, and children's gaming system were gone. You worked many hours for those things and their loss hurts not only yourself but also your innocent children. Imagine the life lesson those two young children would learn. Life is no longer safe for them. Their home has been violated, and they no longer feel safe within the best sanctuary on the planet—their bedrooms. Instead of the ever-vibrant outlook and eager exploration that young children exhibit, you see your children learning fear and uncertainty right before your eyes. How would you feel about crime? How would you feel about punishment? How would you vote on increased penalty laws for ex-offenders? How forgiving would you actually be after that experience?

Consider this: A heroin addict with a 300-dollar-a-day habit can wake up in the morning unemployed and broke. By the end of the day, they have secured the heroin needed to manage their addiction. They have come up with 300 dollars and have done so from possessing nothing more than their wits. Criminal thinking carries with it some keen survival skills; however, these skills always come at the expense of others. They always create a dysfunctional relationship between the individual and society. In many ways, criminals and addicts are perceived by society as sociopaths incapable of being rehabilitated.

Remember: Your chosen affirmation should be the last thing you say to yourself as you are falling asleep, and the first thought on your mind when you wake up each morning.

A prison sentence of twenty-five years to life is a threat to your survival. If you really look at things logically, a prison sentence of any length is a very real threat to your continued existence as a living human. If you take into consideration hepatitis C, HIV, and tuberculosis—all of which are RAMPANT inside correctional facilities—just the health challenges alone are serious risk factors to your life. When I was a case manager at Pelican Bay State Prison, I and everyone who worked inside those walls had to take a TB test every year due to the high concentration of TB in prison settings. I also had to sign an agreement that I would not be negotiated for if I were ever taken hostage. There are many hardcore sociopaths within prison walls, and they are dangerous to prisoners and staff. This brings me to another prison survival challenge: violence.

Gang violence rules the daily life of correctional staff and inmates. A prison is a small city that you really do not want to call home. Within prison walls dwell a diverse group of potentially violent people. You have the Nuestra Familia, MS-13, Mexican Mafia, Aryan Brotherhood, Nazi Low-riders, Fresno Bulldogs, Crips, Bloods, Black Guerrilla Family, Zulu Spear, Hell's Angels, Pagans, and Texas Syndicate. These are just a few of the major groups that can make violence a daily fact of life within a prison. Prison violence—potentially all violence—is based on false mental constructs. False constructs create dysfunctional relationships between people. These false constructs then become dominated by thoughts of racism, control, and perceived power or lack thereof. These are all false constructs, and it is your task to begin dismantling them. There are riots and contracted hits every day in prisons and jails all over America. Injuries and deaths due to racial violence are a sad fact of life within (and also outside of) prison walls.

The first challenge for you to attempt is the challenge of overcoming racism. Subtle or blatant, overt, or covert, racism is an institutional and societal reality. Racism is made even more malevolent by the incarceration process. Prison life demands racial segregation of and by the inmates. Prison staff reinforce this racial divide due to the security challenges of having races mix. Banding together by race and culture helps prisoners feel safer within prison confines. Your first challenge is to consider the false construct of race and how racial identity conflicts may harm your interactions with society. Racism, even subtle racism, can cut you off from major life experiences. It can stop you from meeting beautiful people of all races—people who might have become friends, mentors, and guides. Racism can harm workplace relationships and even impact your own family members. Racism is a false construct, and as you reenter society once again, it is time to let it go. The word "race" should really be replaced with the word "culture" as this would actually be more accurate. We only have one true race—the human race—but we have many cultures. Homo sapiens tend to be molded by the culture into which they are born. This can be both helpful and challenging when it comes to understanding each other. More on this in chapter four. For now, just allow the idea of one human race to take root in your mind like a seed for the tree of life.

Next, consider the concept of fear-based thinking.

Prison life reinforces fear-based thinking. When you are sent to prison, you face fear. Incarceration is designed to make that happen. The first fear is survival; you have to actually consider the question of how to live and not become a casualty. The fear of being injured eventually encourages other fears to manifest. The fear of not living up to your potential, the fear of letting others down, the fear of losing your family's love, the fear of not mattering to anyone anymore. The fear of never accomplishing anything worthwhile. Overshadowing it all is the fear of death. Racism is based on fear. In the free world, you need to let fear-based thinking go. It cannot serve your highest good.

I am going to suggest something radical right now. You may resist this idea initially, but hopefully, you will come around to my way of thinking by the end of this book. I want you to begin to trust yourself. I want you to begin nurturing hope. I want you to begin learning to trust yourself to make better decisions. I want you to examine your thoughts. Let's begin with what makes an affirmation. In order to understand a positive affirmation and how it works, let's first examine negative self-talk. Most people think negative self-talk is only comprised of self-directed put-downs. They think negative self-talk involves internal statements like "I am a loser," "I hate myself," or "why am I so stupid?" This can be true, but in prison, negative self-talk works on an entirely different and destructive level.

Negative self-talk in prison also consists of internal false narratives like: "This bitch needs his ass beat" or "Nobody talks, everybody walks." Or my favorite: "Stay ready so you don't have to get ready." This toxic negative self-talk creates a "them" and "us" continuum that always leads to conflict. The co-occurring anger and fear within these negative affirmations guarantee a path to violence. Just as positive affirmations prepare you for positive experiences and interactions, negative affirmations work on the assumption that you must prepare for negative interactions coming your way. Negative affirmations become self-fulfilling prophecies. In prison, you become an expert in negative self-talk. Negative self-talk is everywhere within prison walls. Your fellow inmates (and even some correctional staff) regale each other with war stories. But that is all they are: stories—bullshit—mostly lies and exaggerations. They are ego constructs intended to make a fear-dominated situation less devastating. Negative self-talk is like a Band-Aid on an amputation.

Negative self-talk allows you to ignore your helplessness in prison or jail. Negative self-talk cannot sustain anyone. You must learn to replace negative self-talk with positive self-talk. This is why you need consciously thought-out positive affirmations. You must counter your conditioned negative self-talk with positive self-talk. Examples of positive affirmations are: "I look for the good in people" or "I enjoy working on myself." I have put enough on you for now. We will address this in more detail later in this book. For now, just let the idea of negative self-talk and positive self-talk sink in. Let the "seeds" get planted and do not disturb them. Let them sprout. Water them by paying attention to your thoughts. This is one of the hardest things you will ever do. Baby steps. Do not worry—just keep reading. You will invalidate your old way of being in the world by attaining new growth.

Remember: Your chosen affirmation should be the last thing you say to yourself as you are falling asleep, and the first thought on your mind when you wake up each morning.

If you have avoided prison so far or made it through prison to parole or probation, then you are to be commended because you are a survivor. You may not have considered making it through the criminal justice system as a survival challenge, but it is. You have a powerful skill, for you have proven that you can adapt and survive. You can also survive probation and parole. You can survive in society. Survival is a matter of gaining the skills you need and recognizing the skills you have at your disposal. It is also a matter of considering new information and adapting to change. Changes in perception can require letting go of old, outdated patterns of being in the world.

Stop lying to yourself if you are doing life on the installment plan. Start thinking like a survivor. Remember, *Webster's New World Dictionary, Third College Edition*, defines survival as: "the act, state, or fact of surviving." Let's review a bit. (Remember this?) It goes on to define survival as: "something or someone who survives." Researching a bit further in Webster's you will find the word "survive." The definition of surviving I like best is: "to continue to live after or in spite of." The example used in Webster's is: "to continue to live after, or in spite of, a shipwreck." If you are in prison, in jail, or on parole or probation, your life is officially a "shipwreck." You are not sailing through life; you are sinking. Worse still you are crashing upon the rocks of the criminal justice system. No ship ever created can sail upon rocks and remain afloat. Your first challenge is to understand that you are in a survival situation while on parole or probation. You must "continue to live after or in spite of" the trauma of conviction, parole, or probation.

Chapter One Exercise

Go to your local library, your institution library, or go online and look up your state's offender laws.

Is your state a three-strikes state? Is your state a one-strike state? What additional penalties do repeat offenders face in your state? You must be honest about your current survival situation. If you continue to commit crime, your physical and mental well-being will suffer. Your loved ones will suffer along with you. They do time when you do time. Remember that fact. Parole and probation violations are nothing to be taken lightly. Avoid them and move into freedom.

Chapter One Essay Question

Use a separate sheet of paper to write out your response.

How do these penal code sections affect my life?

You should include what you want out of life and what you want for your family and those who care about you. Remember to be honest about your current situation. If you are on probation, state parole, federal parole, or are still incarcerated, make sure to include these challenges in your essay. It is important to write this out because you need to slow down your thoughts and start developing a plan for thriving and not just surviving. Don't worry about being perfect the first time around. Just relax, take a deep breath, and write.

Remember that you are not internally defined by your current situation. You are much more than just a disembodied judgment enforced by prison, parole, or probation. You are a human being. Your past only defines you if you allow it to do so. You are much more than your past. You only have control over today, and that is true for everyone—not just people in prison or on parole. Your challenges with allowing the past to control your present moment reality is a battle common to all people. The past is over and cannot be changed. The future has not yet arrived. The present is all anyone has any control over. Whether you are a free person or incarcerated, your present will affect your future. Believe that. Your present will affect your family's future, also. If you continue to commit crime, you can reliably guess what your future will bring. So here is my next bit of advice:

STOP COMMITTING CRIME.

Continued crime is not in your best interest. Crime has a really lousy retirement plan. It has a well-documented history of not working out very well. I am always dumbfounded at inmates and parolees who keep on doing the same thing and expecting a different result. (That's Einstein's definition of insanity.)

Chapter One Personal Development Questions

Use a separate sheet of paper to write out your answers.

1. *Do you have a favorite holiday that means more to you than any other holiday?*
2. *Why is this holiday so meaningful to you?*
3. *How has institutional racism impacted your life inside prison?*
4. *How will racism hinder your new growth?*

More Questions

Next, write out your answer to the following two questions carefully and use as many pages in your notebook as you need in order to be thorough and honest with yourself.

Remember this earlier example? Reconsider it—seriously reconsider it. "Imagine that you come home one day after picking up your children from daycare. Your house has been broken into, and your TV, stereo, and children's gaming system were gone. You worked many hours for those things, and their loss hurts not only yourself but also your innocent children. Imagine the life lesson those two young children would learn. Life is no longer safe for them, their home has been violated, and they no longer feel safe within the best sanctuary on the planet—their bedrooms. Instead of the ever-vibrant outlook and eager exploration that young children exhibit, now you see your children learning fear and uncertainty right before your eyes."

Answer the following two questions honestly.

1. *How would you feel about crime?*
2. *How would you feel about punishment?*

Chapter One Affirmations

1. *I am the child of a beneficent universe and as such, I am a universal being.*
2. *I look for positive possibilities in all interactions.*

Why affirmations? There are a few really good reasons why you need positive affirmations. First, you need to gain control over your thoughts. This is a serious goal. Your thoughts have created your reality. Your internal dialog matters because it directs your decisions. You did not wake up suddenly on parole or probation; you worked at it and your thoughts led you to your current reality.

Second, you need to change your behavior and learn to think in your own rational self-interest. You do this by countering negative self-talk with positive affirmations. Eventually, with enough work and attention, you will regain the ability to think positively and have hope for a better way of life.

Third, affirmations, both positive and negative, will direct your subconscious mind toward positive or negative choices. You may not have considered all the positive possibilities available to you due to an internal dialog of negativity. Positive affirmations will allow you to regain some control over your core subconscious beliefs. Your internal dialog will change, and you will embrace a more positive outlook.

CHAPTER TWO

Choices

If you are using this workbook, then you are (1) currently in prison and getting close to parole, (2) on parole, or (3) on probation or furlough. You may also be a concerned family member of someone who is currently incarcerated. You may feel incarcerated in some ways right along with them. As such, you may be seeking answers that will help both sides. I advise you to not think of this workbook as another "program." Prison systems love "programs." There are work programs, tough love programs, even warm-and-fuzzy programs like working with puppies and listening to audiobooks. After over twenty years of working with prisoners and parolees, I know one thing all too well, programs generally fail. I have seen prisoners and parolees fail in program after program, and I have seen prisoners with no programs succeed. They make their release date, they gain employment, they engage successfully with their community, they find meaning in life, and they never come back. I have seen this rarely but also repeatedly. Your situation in prison has very little to do with your success or failure in life.

This workbook is a resource—a guide, a map—to a new way of thinking and being in the world. Use this workbook to grow in a new and healthy, life-affirming direction. You are at a crossroads now, and you cannot continue living the old way without inviting in more suffering. You cannot live the old way and not bring suffering into the lives of those who care about you. The best way to change your old way of being in the world is to grow in a new direction. The best way to grow in a new direction is to examine your thoughts, your thought processes, your expectations, and your assumptions about the world in which you live.

Old, outdated, dangerous thoughts become old, outdated, negative habits. New, positive, life-affirming thoughts become, over time, new, positive, life-affirming habits. This is a universal principle that you must learn in order to create a new way of being in the world. This will take some sincere effort on your part. It took time for those old, outdated, negative thoughts to become dangerous, freedom-crushing habits. You will have to put in the work to change your thinking, but the rewards are AWESOME. You will have to choose to grow in new directions. You have the innate ability to replace every one of your negative habits with positive ones. You are what you choose to become, and you can become a changed person if that is what you truly desire.

Rehabilitation is just a passing thought—meaningless letters forming a meaningless word if you do not make a conscious choice to commit to positive change. Growth can be painful, and you will have to release some things from your old life that were once comfortable. Survival can be painful. No one ever said survival is a painless process. Right now, the criminal justice system has its boot on your neck. You can lie about your situation, or you can free yourself. It is your CHOICE.

A survivor does not expect others to make his or her survival choices. A survivor does not expect others to do the survival work for them. Everything you need is already inside you. It springs from your heart, and it's called desire. Desire leads to choices, and those choices guide your life. You make them in the present moment, from moment to moment, and these choices begin to form your future. What does your past look like? Your past is the result of choices made within a past, long gone moment. Your past reflects the impact of those choices. This is true for everyone facing challenges, it is especially true for people trying to change toxic relationship patterns.

If you have failed to complete parole or probation in the past, you have challenges with relationships. Working with your probation officer is a relationship in progress. Who you hang out with is also a relationship in progress. Interacting with your family, coworkers, and supervisors are all relationships in progress. How successful you are on parole is a direct result of how you interact with people in your community. All of them. You can try to deny this but just remember that your ego is trying to make you right and everyone else wrong.

You can blame your past, your upbringing, the judge, the jury, parents, snitches, friends, friends of friends, or your parole officer—it does not change anything regarding your choices. Your desires led to choices, and those choices have guided and impacted your life. If you refuse to admit this fact of life, then you know your ego is in charge. Your negative life lessons will simply repeat, and your ego will teach you nothing until you let go of it and choose to live a life with purpose.

How do you choose to live a life with purpose?

First, you must find the answers to four questions. We all encounter these questions as we move through life. These are powerful questions to which we seek answers even when we don't realize that we are asking ourselves these questions. In short, these are eternal questions we are all born with.

1. *Who am I?*
2. *What is my purpose?*
3. *What is the meaning of life?*
4. *Is there life after death?*

Although I am just an old-fashioned chemical dependency counselor, I ask all my clients these questions eventually because they are important questions to ask. Your willingness to answer them honestly will test your ability to find meaning and purpose in life. Indeed, the answers to these questions will affect all your future choices and lead to the only true freedom there is, living a purpose-driven life. These answers are crucial for your continued freedom and your success or failure on parole or probation. A purpose-driven life cannot fail, but a life without purpose fails before it even begins. We will address these questions in depth a little later, so until then, file them away in the back of your mind and let your subconscious work on them a bit.

Sometimes it is hard to recognize purpose. When you were serving time in prison, your basic humanity was under constant assault. This is a natural consequence of the incarceration process. To survive in the concrete and steel world of disease, violence, rape, criminal thinking, and negativity, you gained an important survival skill: denial. Inmates and ex-felons become experts in denial. Psychologically, you had to deny your lack of power and choice in your day-to-day life as a prisoner because your ability to influence and change your circumstances was severely impaired. Rather than admit your powerlessness, you lived in denial. You had no choice in your clothing; you wore what you were told to wear. You had no choice in food; you ate what was cooked and served. You read the books that were approved by your institution and allowed within the prison library. You watched "approved" movies, and if you had TV, it was most likely in a day room airing only "approved" channels and shows. The noise pollution was a relentless and daily assault on your conscious mind. You experienced not only a lack of *freedom of choice* but, ironically, you also experienced *freedom from choice*. You adapted to having *freedom from choice*, and you began to think it was *freedom of choice*.

During your period of captivity, your naked body was searched by strangers—down to your body cavities. You had to squat and spread your butt cheeks for a stranger, so he or she could literally look inside your rectum. You had to open your mouth and let them inspect your throat, inside your cheeks, and under your tongue. You used a toilet and showered in front of other people. Inside your concrete cage, you defecated less than three feet away from the steel bunk of other cell partners.

On the yard, you paraded around like a tough guy, like a so-called badass. You took the clothes they made you wear, and you changed some things: maybe rolled up your sleeves or made cuffs on your jeans. You talked endlessly with other "cons" about respect and honor. You became great at puffing up in front of the right and safe people and staying cool and calm around the wrong and dangerous people. All the while, you were a champion of denial.

You had no privacy, no respect, and no honor. You were powerless to do anything other than submit to the will of prison authorities, still, you thought you were tough. You couldn't buy a steak or have sex with your significant other, but you let yourself think you had gained respect. You could have tattoos made with illegal and possibly infectious prison-made tattoo guns. You could break the rules and not get caught. You could even smoke the occasional joint filled with weed that someone smuggled inside the prison in their rectum. All for an inflated price. Yes, the rectum is the chosen mode of goods transportation in prison. Within the rectum, inmates can bring in heroin, needles, cocaine, amphetamine, and of course, weapons. All available for a price and continued negative contracts.

A typical negative contract in recovery entails using drugs with a so-called friend while in rehab, or keeping secrets about others using drugs. In recovery, negative contracts will destroy your sobriety. They will take your freedom in prison and on parole. Negative contracts are not real friendships. They are not true bonds of shared experience even though they are shared secrets that may feel like bonds. The only things they bond you to are danger, criminality, and dysfunction. All exchanges done with negative contracts are done in championship-level denial.

I understand that your life depends on staying quiet in prison. I do insist, however, that you stay honest with yourself about your reality. Prison helped you become an expert in ignoring how disgusting prison life actually is in practice. None of it entailed actual respect, friendship, freedom, or power. Everyone was using someone for something. You were only choosing from finite and limited choices. You did not have *freedom of choice*—you had *freedom from choice*. You were in denial, and you were powerless. You couldn't even turn off your lights at night. You had a bedtime like a child. Until those lights came back on, and someone opened your cage at the allotted time, you could not shower. You had to urinate and defecate next to where you and your cell partner slept. Not even animals do that.

Your ego, utilizing the power of denial, helped you survive. Instead of seeing the reality of your unmanageable life and unwise choices, you convinced yourself that you were honorable and people respected you. Everything was someone else's fault, and you were a victim. You obeyed the so-called convict code and you were tough. You told yourself that you "stayed ready" so you would not have to "get ready." It was all an unpleasant fiction—an effort in delusion. In truth, it is easy to tell if your ego is in charge of your thinking. Your ego will convince you that everyone else is wrong, and you are always right. The ego will do this despite the horrible truth and circumstances of your reality.

You behaved like a sociopath because you were immersed in a criminal culture that supported and affirmed lawlessness. This is the core of prison culture, and it is also the core of addiction culture. Remember that prison friendships are almost always negative contracts.

Coming from the substance abuse model, I am big on recognizing negative contracts. A negative contract is when two or more people agree both consciously or subconsciously to keep a secret that may be harmful to others or dangerous to all people involved. In chemical dependency counseling, we run into this challenge as people learn to avoid staying enmeshed within the toxic culture of addiction. Past friends and associates who do not value sobriety are especially dangerous to someone seeking a life of sobriety. You also have a toxic culture in which you are enmeshed, the culture of criminality. Your past choices in friends and associates can make or break your current attempts at obtaining real freedom. Old friends and associates can destroy your chances of successful parole.

The sociopath's motto is: "Laws don't apply to me."

The sociopath's slogan is: "I didn't do it." (Evidence does not matter.)

The sociopath's oath is: "If I did it, I have a good reason and you should leave me alone about it."

I am not calling you a sociopath. I am just pointing out observations that parole officers (and others) make. At some point in time, you learned to look out for yourself at the expense of others. You may have become excellent at denying all responsibility for your choices or decisions. You may have learned to manipulate others. You may have accepted your reality of *freedom from choice*. The culture of criminality is a lot like the culture of addiction. Everyone is out for themselves, and relationships are tools for accomplishing dysfunctional false goals. People, places, and things can put your freedom at risk in the same way that they can put sobriety at risk.

YOU MADE DECISIONS BASED ON LIMITED CHOICES.

PRIVACY is something taken for granted by free people. To invade the privacy of a free person can incite rage. Over the unstoppable march of time, inmates gradually accept privacy violations because they have no choice. In a two-person cell, you and your partner urinated, defecated, snored, and dressed in front of each other and correctional staff—sometimes for years.

You learned what blood, semen, unwashed bodies, nasty feet, and fecal matter smelled like because those are daily smells within prison walls. You came to accept this limited and unpleasant worldview the same way that all people with limited circumstances come to accept ugliness—gradually. While living in denial, you gradually learned to accept your lack of control and choice. You finally became an inmate and ceased to be a person. If you do not learn to see things as they are, if you fail to see how choices are important and how they make change happen over time, you will stay incarcerated. If you stay in denial and remain a slave to your ego, making everyone else wrong and you always right, you will stay an inmate. The universe is challenging your personhood. Take the challenge. See probation and parole as an opportunity and not a punishment. Change is the immutable law of the universe. Parole and probation can become vehicles for healthy change, or they can become a revolving door.

Remember: allowing your ego to rule your choices leads only to despair. You will falsely believe that everyone else is wrong, and you are always right. You will win every battle, but lose the ultimate war for your freedom. Even when you are free of the criminal justice system, you will still be an inmate. You will think like an inmate and act like an inmate. You will eventually return to the place where inmates live out their lives—a world of steel cages, cement, and championship-level sociopaths. All of this will reflect your choices.

When you finally realize that you have freedom of choice, CHOOSE WISELY.

The major reason for parole and probation violations, without exception, is simple: you choose to violate. You choose to not follow the rules. Your criminal thinking errors, polished by years of incarceration, have hijacked your worldview. On parole, you will be faced with many new choices, and you may have lost the ability to see positive possibilities. Years of *freedom from choice* have left you unable to cope with *freedom of choice*.

You need to learn how to be in the world again. You must relearn what it is to be a free individual in society, and you will have to relearn it from the ground up. Start by making healthy, proactive choices. In prison and within criminal culture, you learned to react to many negative situations that sprung up uninvited all around you. You never realized that your choices put you into the many situations you were reacting to, nor did you realize that your choices could separate you from those situations. Your choices can change your life positively or negatively. Change will always happen, either due to your positive choices or negative choices.

The rules in the free world are different from the rules in prison. Your best chance for survival is to think, consider, and choose wisely before you react to anything. Survivors do not lie about their tactical situation. Denial was a survival game that your ego came up with to help you survive in prison. In the free world, denial is just a fancy way of lying to yourself. Your mind is your most valuable asset in your quest to thrive in the free world. You must learn to use your mind differently. Denial helped you cope with the hopelessness and ugliness of prison life. Denial can also result in twenty-five years to life back in prison when you are on parole in a world loaded with *freedom of choice*. You must discard that outdated, ego-driven survival skill of denial leftover from prison life. You must replace that skill with a new, free-world survival skill: self-honesty.

Chapter Two Personal Development Questions

Answer the following questions and take all the time you need to think about them.

1. *Who am I?*
2. *What is my purpose?*
3. *What is the meaning of life?*
4. *Is there life after death?*
5. *What does freedom mean to you? (I do not mean getting released from jail or prison, probation, or parole; I mean living as a free person.)*

These are important questions. For some people, incarceration, and probation/parole has become a way of life—an accepted way of being in the world. To change your past way of life, you must invalidate this cycle by growing in new directions. You can no longer tolerate old relationships that jeopardize your freedom or sabotage your new growth. You simply cannot continue to interact with the culture of criminality any longer. This includes negative contracts between dysfunctional family members, former associates, and so-called friends. You cannot choose your family, but you can choose to not allow family dysfunction to slap you with twenty-five years to life behind bars due to harsh sentencing laws. You can choose to not associate with past crime partners, drug users, and people still embroiled in a criminal lifestyle and enmeshed in the culture of criminality or, oftentimes, addiction. People whose egos run their choices will always make someone else wrong and themselves right, no matter what the evidence or circumstances reveal otherwise. These are people who only use others for gain. The drug dealer is not your friend, and neither is your crime partner. These outdated, toxic relationships are unhealthy diversions that lead back to the steel cage. So now, your goal is to find new role models. You need new, true friends that will teach you some new skills. Humans learn from other humans and a role model is someone you choose to emulate, so choose wisely. Future change will always happen because of your present moment choices, whether they be negative, positive, or neutral ones.

You are who you choose to become.

Here are my own answers to the above questions:

1. *Who am I?*
    I am a being-becoming. I am a child of the universe, and I am learning and growing always.

2. *What is my purpose?*

    My purpose is to serve and to help others realize the truth of who they are and the truth of their being. To do this, I must continue to learn and grow, to share as much as I can with my fellow Earthtribe brothers and sisters.

3. *What is the meaning of life?*

    The meaning of life is to learn the lessons of life with humility, grace, and poise. (I am still working hard on this.)

4. *Is there life after death?*

    Nothing our planet creates ever goes away; it only changes forms. When a bonfire is lit, the logs do not vanish, rather, they change from a solid to a gas. They release the energy that the sun gave to the tree. For me, the spiritual principle of "as above, so below" holds true. I come from a Divine Source—I am a spiritual being having physical experiences. Thus, when my body has served its divine purpose, my spirit will move on to new lessons. My lessons will continue until they are all learned. Then more lessons will follow.

5. *What does freedom mean to you? (I don't mean getting released from jail or prison, probation, or parole; I mean living as a free person.)*

    Freedom lies in the sure knowledge that we are never separate from our true Source. We cannot be separate from our Source, for we are all of that which has created us. We are divine beings, for we are created from a Divine Source. Duality and separation from this Source is an illusion. It is the grandest illusion, for it has kept us divided for centuries. Recognizing that we and our Source are one frees us from the two-camp continuum of "them" and "us." It ends the concept of the dog-eat-dog world. It releases us from hatred, racism, intolerance, and the illusion that we must take from others because there is not enough to go around. When you know with certainty that you are the child of an unlimited Source, a Source that creates unlimited multiverses, you know that you have all that you ever need. Furthermore, you are led to a life of service to others, for in serving others you serve Source and thus align yourself with Source (this cannot be otherwise.) This is true freedom. This is the only true freedom, for all else is an illusion that eventually enslaves.

> *"Allowing your ego to rule your choices leads only to despair. Everyone else will be wrong, and you will always be right. You will win every battle and lose the ultimate war for your freedom. Even when you are free of the criminal justice system, you will be an inmate. You will think like an*

inmate and act like an inmate. You will eventually return to the place where inmates live out their lives. A world of steel cages, cement, and championship-level sociopaths. All of it will reflect your choices."
—Dante B. Kun

For you created my inmost being
> you knit me together in my mother's womb.

I praise you because I am fearfully and wonderfully made;
> your works are wonderful,
> I know that full well.

My frame was not hidden from you
> when I was made in the secret place,
> when I was woven together in the depths of the earth.

Your eyes saw my unformed body;
> all the days ordained for me were written in your book
> before one of them came to be.

Ps. 139:13–16. *The King James Bible*

Chapter Two Exercise

Research positive, successful people and pick one as a hypothetical role model and mentor.

After you have learned all that you can about them, imagine they are giving you advice and life coaching. What would they say to you? What would they focus on? Write two pages of the advice and coaching they would give you. Be specific about the challenges in your life that they would address. You can pick anyone you want, living or dead, from Lincoln to Gandhi.

This exercise is important. You are beginning to flex your mind like you flex your muscles. You are developing your *freedom of choice* muscle. You choose this role model, you choose these core values, and you make it all work. It is always your "response-ability" (meaning, your ability to respond) that impacts your life for better or worse. You must find what works for you. No one else can do that for you. You are unique, and your challenges are unique to you. No one else is going to figure it out better than you. Free life is a series of constantly changing situations that call for decision-making. Indeed, free life is a constant and ongoing process of decision-making. It is no longer in your best interest to allow former associates, crime partners, or toxic relationships to dictate those decisions.

CHOOSE WISELY.

If you have expectations that a program can make decisions for you, you are doomed to fail. You are circumventing responsibility and the possible difficulty involved in choosing for yourself. You are expecting others to make your survival decisions. This is always a bad idea.

A role model is someone you admire for their habits, core values, and ethics. Role models can become a road map to a better life by emulating their habits, but know that you will most likely not duplicate everything about them, their actions, or their lifestyle. It is your responsibility to find that job, school, training, therapy, relationship, or program that will work best for you and your unique situation. Then you must work at it. Change—for better or for worse—happens as a direct result of your choices. You are who you choose to become. Einstein's definition of insanity was to do the same thing over and over expecting a different result. Please don't do that.

> "It is not the strongest of the species that survive, nor the most intelligent, but the one most responsive to change."
> —Charles Darwin

Chapter Two Affirmations

1. *I love myself for I am love.*
2. *I share love with all around me for the Universe and I are one.*

CHAPTER THREE

Guilt, Anger, Regret

GUILT

You choose to feel guilt.

I call the emotions of guilt, anger, and regret, The Big Three to my clients in recovery. I name them this because they have destroyed many lives, and I have great respect for their ability to wreck lives. Most people—and not just those on parole—feel lost when it comes to The Big Three. Deep down, I bet you think that you have no control over your emotions. You think your emotions are "you." That is not correct. Let's examine guilt. When you live in guilt, you live in the past, bound to the past by choices you have already made. Decisions you made that brought about results or consequences. The aftermath of past decisions has long since played out. You cannot change those decisions you made in the past nor the results of those past decisions. You have grown and learned new information. Those choices and decisions taught you life lessons and influenced your life and present circumstances, but you do not have to stay bound up in the past. By making new choices today you will create a new future. You most likely would not make the same choices today that you made in years past if faced with identical circumstances currently. Your choices right now will influence your life in the future.

Guilt is a secondary emotion.

You remember your past decision. You remember the result of that decision. Then, you suddenly feel guilty. The thoughts of your past came first, then guilt. Guilt is a useless emotion at this stage in your life. No one can change the past. Since we know that this is not possible, it makes no sense to dwell in the past. If you feel guilt, there is one positive aspect, at least you know you are not a true sociopath and you can learn. Just remember that in the long run, guilt does nothing to foster new growth. There will come a time when you must let it go. This happens for us all.

Many people are under the impression that prisons are giant country clubs. They think you enjoyed many privileges and opportunities while incarcerated. Do not expect free society to understand your situation. Do not allow yourself to fall into resentment due to other people's perceptions. Do not fall into the guilt trap due to their judgments of your past. Their reality is not yours, and your reality is not theirs. They did not make your choices, so do not allow guilt from an unchangeable past to influence your choices today. In fact, no one has the power to make you feel anything. You possess the power to choose how you feel. You just may not realize this fact at this moment in time. You have experienced some life lessons due to unwise choices. Now you must accept these lessons and resolve to make healthy choices in the only place where you can do so: the present moment. You only have the present moment to make change and better decisions. I repeat: You cannot change the past. You are not yet in the future. You have only this moment. Use this moment well.

Once you realize and accept the true strength that you have over your emotions and thoughts you will experience great internal freedom. If you allow yourself to succumb to the secondary emotion of guilt, you are on the road to hopelessness. You are on the road back to prison. You are still mentally an inmate. You are still in the past, experiencing your old, outdated past choices. You are not accepting the lessons learned here within the present moment.

There is a power in not allowing guilt to control your actions and behavior. It is a human superpower to be able to choose wisely and not allow emotion to hijack your choices. I encourage my clients in recovery to tap into their ability to choose their actions in this present moment, free of guilt. Every human has this power, and some use it to completely change the direction of their lives. I like to use the story of Paul to illustrate the power of not allowing guilt to keep you stuck on an old path that cannot serve your highest good.

The apostle Paul was once named Saul. Saul was a mass murderer and a violent man. Had he allowed guilt and his unchangeable past to define him—and thus rule his present moment choices—he would never have made it off the road to Damascus. He would never have transformed and thus allowed the truth of his Divine Source and Being-Becoming to manifest and become Paul. Had he chosen to succumb to guilt from past life choices that no longer represented his new growth and direction he would not have transformed. Instead of learning from past errors in thinking and perception, he never would have written anything, much less become an apostle of Jesus. His writing inspires people today to make positive life choices. His writing is a direct result of his ability to embrace a new way of being in the world, a new life, and new choices. Paul became a new man due to his choices. He could no longer be separate from his Divine Source. He left Saul behind because his old way of life was invalidated by the demands of new growth required for his Being-Becoming. He had free will, and he used it. If Saul can choose to listen to Source and leave behind a life of mass-murdering and hatred to become the truth of his being, out-picturing his Divine Source through himself as Paul, you too can leave your past behind. Such is the transformative power of Divine Source. Use your free will and choose wisely. You can become an entirely new person. Others have done exactly this, and so can you.

You are not your past.

Your past is an ancient reflection of old choices invalidated by new growth within the present moment. Know this without a doubt. You are neither your past nor your past decisions; you are much more than those old situations. Your life lessons have taught you a lot, and if you have been paying attention, they have enriched your ability to make healthy choices. Prison was a punishment as well as a learning experience. Some choices were made for you by others—judges, lawyers, prison staff, parole officers, juries—your life was managed by others. Control was taken from you. Your relationships with your family and loved ones suffered because of the incarceration process. This was a direct result of old choices you made long ago in your distant past. Thus, your family suffered with you as you went through the incarceration process and its resulting life lessons. You cannot change past decisions within the present moment. You can only change present moment choices.

You cannot change the past or how past choices and decisions have affected you and those you love. There is only one healthy path open to you right now in this present moment: change the way you live in the present by making healthy new choices. All your healthy choices right now are creating a positive future that is yet unknown to you. Society has removed its chunk of flesh, Lady Justice has balanced the scales, and the judge has banged the gavel. It's time to move on. You have survived prison—now survive parole. Choose to thrive, not just survive.

You are who you choose to become.

You are not your past choices.

ANGER

Anger is another useless and secondary emotion. You are not your anger, and yet you choose to become angry. You allow anger to manifest. Anger, more than all other emotions combined, has sent people right back to prison with alarming regularity. If you are in a prerelease class or under parole/probation supervision, anger can stop your release, crush your plans, ruin your life, and eliminate your freedom forever. Anger can absolutely crush your life and alter your life path.

You are not your anger.

You choose to be angry.

The following exercises will help you deal with anger.

Releasing the Debt Exercise

Almost all words have multiple definitions. One definition of forgiveness is "to let go of the debt." Many former and current inmates have a hard time with forgiveness, especially if it involves forgiving someone who abused or neglected them. In the case of childhood abuse, many survivors carry around deep-seated resentment, anger, and a sense of having had something stolen from them. The underlying feeling that the abuser owes them something—perhaps a childhood, for example.

If someone owed you fifty thousand dollars, you would want to be compensated. If you hunted them down for years, and finally found them in a gutter, wearing rags, barefoot and homeless, could you collect that fifty thousand? No. If you feel that your parents owed you a childhood, and you never experienced a childhood, can you collect that childhood today? No. Letting go of the debt can be the healthiest "selfish" thing that you can do. Carrying around a sense of loss, resentment, anger—even hatred—only hurts your health and relationships. It saps your vital energy and lowers your ability to live life to its fullest. Write out your answers to the questions below. Use another sheet of paper if needed.

Remember: Choices are everywhere, and choices impact the future as well as the present. Allowing your ego to rule your choices will lead only to despair. When the ego rules, everyone else is wrong, and only you are right. Living this way, you may win every battle, but you will lose the ultimate war for your freedom. Even when you are free of the criminal justice system, you will be an inmate. You will think like an inmate and act like an inmate. You will eventually return to the place where inmates live out their lives. Your mental state will reflect your choices.

Answer the following questions honestly:

1. *Has something been taken you cannot ever recover? Describe what you lost.*
2. *How much time per day do you think about your loss? Does this help or change anything?*
3. *If you could go back in time and change things, what would you change?*
4. *How would you be different?*
5. *How would you be the same?*
6. *What baggage are you carrying every day over this debt?*
7. *How will you feel without this baggage weighing on your mind?*

Read everything you have written out loud or quietly to yourself. Then, burn your answer sheet (if possible) and release the debt—lighten your load. Repeat as needed.

Your past is an ancient reflection of old choices invalidated by new growth in the present moment.

The Haiku Exercise

This is one of my favorite exercises. It can be done solo or in a group. I use it in substance abuse counseling. It is very useful to anyone personally struggling with relationship challenges because it helps to slow racing thoughts. It also helps with managing the "chemical cascade" of overwhelming emotions. This exercise will bring your subconscious into play. In substance abuse counseling this exercise is especially useful to help people in recovery leave the toxic culture of addiction. The exercise brings awareness to the personal cost of negative contracts and toxic interactions. If you are on parole, you are in a relationship challenge with yourself and society. We are social creatures, and our interpersonal relationships are important for our well-being.

Haiku is a form of Japanese poetry. A traditional form of Japanese Haiku consists of a three-line poem. The first line has only five syllables, the second line has seven syllables, and the third line has five syllables. Here is one of my Haiku as an example:

> One moon together
> Forever in time it stays
> Constant as one love

The samurai used to write haiku to strengthen, balance, and calm their minds. They believed that the constraints of the syllabic form created a strength of mind that gave the writer more creative ability. Your assignment is to use the haiku form to encapsulate a source of anger or conflict trigger. Once that is done, you will use the same form to encapsulate a peaceful solution. Finally, you will create a haiku that conveys a peaceful concept, idea, or scene. The scene can be from nature, the ocean, a garden, the weather, or any peaceful image you can imagine. When you are done, you will have a nine-line poem. Here is my poem as an example:

> Your rage shakes my house
> And my rage, uncaged, begins
> Where can I find peace?
> I know your resin
> Exists not in my forest
> Peace is within me

> *My ocean glistens*
> *My moonlight universal*
> *My sky eternal*

The haiku exercise will, over time, strengthen your ability to contemplate and focus. Both are useful and essential skills in managing anger and conflict. If you are in a prerelease class, the first half of the class will be spent quietly, creating our individual haikus. There will be no talking, just contemplation, and creation. During the second half, we will share our haikus and the concepts within them. If you are doing this solo, follow the silence rule as you create. Turn off your phone, your computer, and your TV. Do this alone if possible. All healthy solutions require some contemplation beforehand. This exercise is one I encourage you to use throughout your life. The contemplation of healthy solutions requires practice.

The Resentment Exercise

The resentment exercise is meant to help group participants or individuals begin to forgive. I have found that a lot of my clients struggle with forgiveness because they don't understand the forgiveness dynamic. They are hurt and angry and see forgiveness as weak. Most people who are chronically angry give too much of their own personal power to people or situations they resent. They let people "rent space in their mind," when they could be using that space to focus on their own happiness, creative projects, dreams, or people close to them—or to just be inspired by life.

The path to forgiveness entails three important steps:

1. *Your first challenge is to attain radical self-honesty.* This will take a lot of hard work. In recovery work, we refer to radical self-honesty as telling the truth even when it hurts. Dishonesty in recovery is always a source of stress. When you can face your own dishonesty head-on, even when facing the harsh truth is embarrassing or painful, you will be happier. Radical self-honesty works on the universal principle that true self-actualization is just not possible when you continue to hide things from yourself. It is in your rational self-interest to tell the truth to yourself.

Acknowledge your true feelings about the situation that causes your resentment. Is the source of your resentment and hatred due to a "debt" that can never be repaid? Are you angry over a childhood that can never be lived out? Are you being dishonest with yourself about how you truly feel? Are you denying your resentment and continuing to stay in contact with people who do not support your growth or well-being? Are you fueling your resentment by denying your past choices? Are you fueling your anger by focusing on the negative choices of others?

2. *Recognize your role in maintaining the resentment and the co-occurring personal cost.* Be honest about how much energy this requires on your part. Realize that this ongoing, toxic resentment hurts you. The energy you expend on this resentment every day is energy you will never regain. It is energy that will make you bleed out emotionally if you allow the dynamic to continue.

3. *Focus on the benefits of letting the anger and its co-occurring resentment go.* Sometimes long-term anger is frightening to let go of. Especially if it has been your loyal and personal companion, life may seem scary without it at your side. If anger makes you feel strong or powerful, you might feel weak or defenseless without it. But the opposite is the truth. The more energy you invest in long-term anger, the less energy and focus you invest in issues that need your awareness and attention. Anger is not healthy fuel; anger only consumes its vehicle for expression.

You are not your anger.

Your past is an ancient reflection of old choices invalidated by new growth in the present moment.

You are not your past.

The exercise: Have each participant address the three steps in writing quietly as a group. Once they are finished with the questions, each participant checks in and shares their resentment with the group and facilitator for group feedback and advice. If you are doing this exercise solo, just remember to turn off your phone, your computer, and your TV. Do the exercise in a quiet place where you will be undisturbed. Remember, the more resentment and its co-occurring anger you carry around with you each day, the less response-ability to have for life lessons, opportunities, and challenges. Unresolved anger and resentment will stifle your creativity, your communication, your relationships, and your interactions within society. Unresolved anger can send you back to jail or prison. Coming to terms with your anger and resentment toward others is the greatest challenge you will face in maintaining your continued freedom. There is no way to fake this challenge. It is a challenge you must resolve successfully. It will take time and effort, but it is well worth it because you are worth the effort.

You are not your anger. You are not your past. You are not your resentment.

Anger is not healthy fuel; anger only consumes its vehicle for expression.

The Felony Stop Exercise

The path to physical violence has three predictable stages that are recognized by researchers. The verbal phase, the posturing phase, and the physical phase. The verbal and posturing phases are almost always co-occurring. They involve tone of voice, body language, facial expressions, and blended micro-expressions. Researchers agree that over ninety percent of all aggression begins and ends in the verbal and posturing phases of conflict. This role-playing exercise was used at Pelican Bay State Prison in the transitional housing unit to help inmates understand the power that verbal and nonverbal communication manifests in conflict resolution and anger management.

Choices are everywhere, and choices impact the future as well as the present. Your choices in the heat of an unthoughtful moment can be the catalyst that propels you back into a cage. If you allow your secondary emotions to control your thoughts, and those thoughts control your actions, you will be arrested, and you will go back to prison. Someone else's tone of voice or body language belongs to them alone. It is their reality at that moment. Don't make it your reality. Your response is all yours—always. You cannot control what others do and say, but you have total control over what you do and say.

The exercise: Two group participants play the role of cops and two participants play the role of parolees driving a car and stopped by the police. When a person has a felony on their record, it shows up for life. Even if their car is properly registered and legal, the police usually do what is called a "felony stop procedure." This involves calling for backup, having weapons ready, and searching the vehicle. It is generally a stressor event. The police are already within the verbal and posturing phase of violence because felony stops are statistically one of the most lethal for police officers. Felony stops rank close to domestic violence calls in lethal outcomes. If verbal and posturing escalate to unsafe levels, the physical phase is almost always met with violence being the obvious outcome of the conflict.

Two participants pretend to be driving, while one participant is the officer that pulls them over. The officer calls for backup and both officers enter the verbal and posturing phase as they institute the felony stop procedure. They search both occupants and question them aggressively. The driver and passenger use body language, verbal language, "I statements," facial expressions, and tone of voice to communicate in such a way as to de-escalate the situation. Afterward, the group identifies the conflict resolution techniques used in the role-play exercise to make suggestions, comments, and share new ideas on conflict resolution. If you are doing this workbook solo, enlist the help of family or friends to do this exercise.

I have met with many inmates and parolees who carry around anger, resentment, and even unbalanced rage against the criminal justice system. They will claim to HATE their counselors, correctional officers, judges, parole officers, the police who arrested them, their public defenders, and so on. They hate the DAs, the justice system, and the penal system in general. Hate, anger, and resentment have become a regular part of their internal reality. This is unhealthy. This is also championship-level denial.

Anger is a secondary emotion always. You choose to be angry. Your response is all yours—always. You cannot control what others do and say, but you have total control over what you do and say.

The Department of Corrections in any state simply cannot hang out a No Vacancy sign. A judge may have handed down a sentence, but you alone made the choices that landed you in front of the judge. You arrived at the penal system directly because of the choices you made on a certain day and time. No correctional officer or parole officer ever requested your presence within a prison or parole office. Before you showed up, they never knew of your existence. They will not think about you after you leave.

Anger is not healthy fuel; anger only consumes its vehicle for expression.

Chapter Three Questions

1. *Why would you continue to dwell upon them?*
2. *What purpose does it serve?*
3. *How does holding onto resentment fuel your new growth?*
4. *How does anger help you find true purpose in life?*

You can choose to be angry, and you can choose to seek peace. You can choose to let go of anger.

Staying angry at people who work within the penal system is a waste of your precious energy, time, and resources. Energy, time, and resources that can take away from the good time you could be spending with friends and loved ones. Energy, time, and resources that you can use to better your life, fund creative projects, act in your own rational self-interest, and grow in healthier directions. Throughout all this time you have had choices. Many more choices are in store for you. The choices will never stop. Lessons will continue until they are learned.

If you alter your attitude about life, your life will change.

REGRET

Regret is another secondary emotion, and it is also useless. The past is truly dead and over with. You cannot change the past any more than you can time travel. Regret is akin to giving medicine to a corpse and expecting it to work. Regret only hurts your present moment, and that moment in time is the only moment in which you must now make choices. The future has not happened. The past has already happened. Regret has no place in your present moment. Regret cannot help you grow.

Regret is a time bandit. Time is precious, so do not waste a second of it.

You simply do not possess the power to change anything that has already happened. You can make amends. You can see past choices as life lessons and learn from those past choices. You can acknowledge that there are always multiple choices available. You can recognize that in the past you did not see all the choices you had available due to allowing yourself to be led by emotion rather than reason. You can accept that you did not see all the positive possibilities open to you. You can accept responsibility for past choices and learn from those choices, but you cannot change past choices.

Regret is optional, never mandatory.

The words you spoke, the actions you took, the other available choices you did not see or consider—these things are over with. They are done. They are lost to time and not present within the now. They exist only in your mind. Do not let these past situations influence your present choices by blinding you to present positive possibilities. You are not your past; you are much more than that. Look for other choices that are available within the present moment. Your choices today will influence your tomorrow.

The only action you can take in the present moment is to accept the past and its lessons, learn from those lessons, and move on. Any other action allows the past to rule your present moment, and all you have is your present moment. Regret is a time bandit. Don't allow regret to rob you of your present moment in time.

Regret is a secondary emotion, thus you and only you choose regret, to dwell in regret, to lose the present moment, to stay in regret, to make decisions and choices based on regret. Choose instead to stay within the moment always.

Thought is powerful. Everything begins with a thought. My laptop, my cell phone, my truck—these things all started with a thought. Someone first visualized their creation and then brought the vision into being. It all started with a thought, and then it was conceptualized on paper or on a computer. Then it was created. You can observe this process with a 3D printer. Thought is beautiful. You are a thinking being, and you cannot change that. Thought is the start of everything. Thought began your path to incarceration. Likewise, thought is the only way to find or create a new path. Thought can lead you away from future incarceration if you so choose.

Thought can help you stay free.

You will encounter people on your path. Some will be encouraging of your new growth, while some will only want to bring up your past. You cannot control other people's thoughts and actions. Since their words and actions spring from their thoughts, and you are not a mind reader, you will neither be able to see their actions coming nor anticipate their words. When you meet people who judge you by your past, just know that they are living in the past. Refuse to argue with them. Do not try to convince them of anything. It is a waste of time. They are speaking from their ego, and the ego just wants to make everyone wrong and itself right—always. They are trying to bring up your past to make you "wrong" within the present moment. You are not your past.

When you become defensive or argue with them, you are just playing ego games. You are doubting yourself and your present moment choices. You are giving away your personal power by accepting their negativity. You are also living in the past right alongside them. You are losing time in the present, and your energy is focused upon defending your own ego and a dead past. Precious and finite time is better spent on your new growth—your new path. You are squandering your energy on the past. A past that cannot be changed. This is all an exercise in futility. Do not buy into this false construct. The present moment is the best place to use time.

If you want to change other people's opinions, show them rather than argue with them. To be an example requires choice—always.

Do not allow other people's value judgments based on their own ego constructs about your past choices to influence your precious present moments. You are neither your emotions nor your past. Begin using thought to create positive, life-affirming choices that result in a positive, present moment life. This will take some sincere work on your part to not engage negative people. Just know that every time you engage a person who is determined to bring up the past, you are not in the present, and you are allowing them to make you live within the past. Use "I statements" and positive affirmations such as: "I like to live in the present, not the past." "I make better choices now." "I have learned from my past and have accepted the lessons." Then get away from the negative person as fast as you can. Negative thinking takes a toll on you. Guilt, anger, and regret can block you from seeing positive possibilities and choices. You are not your past. The past is dead, and the future is not yet here. Live right now. Make your present moment the place where positive choices are made.

Your response is all yours—always. You cannot control what others do and say, but you have total control over what you do and say within each precious moment in time.

Do not allow other people's value judgments based on their own ego constructs about your past choices to influence your precious present moments. You are neither your emotions nor your past. Begin using thought to create positive, life-affirming choices that result in a positive, present moment life.

Chapter Three Affirmation

1. *I affirm with love and acceptance that I cannot be separate from that which created me.*

CHAPTER FOUR

The Tale of the Earthtribe

I must tell you the tale of our true Mother. The Mother of the Earthtribe. I must tell you who first birthed Her, our Mother, and how she came into being. I must tell you all about the Mother of our Mother. Within this story, you will also learn about the first Mother, our Great-Grandmother Source. This will reveal a long-hidden truth. The truth that we are all one tribe: The Earthtribe.

Once upon a time, there existed a Source of all that is and ever will be. Source has always and will always exist. It exists even right now. For this is the sacred mystery held within the Source of The All. Many have tried to name, classify, and identify Source but all have failed for Source just is and will always be, and it has no name. Source is not nameable because it exists within a thought form that is neither connected to thought by word nor dependent on symbols. It is, thus, unlimited. Source is powerful and mysterious for even the word "unlimited" cannot describe a limitless existence, and all attempts to describe the freedom of Source limits the understanding of Source because it cannot be contained by such descriptions. Source can only be experienced, and never can this experience of Source be explained by those whom it creates. Source cannot be touched, but that which comes from Source can be touched and touch others—though those things from Source come and go and always transform. Sometimes, they transform into the untouchable, only to be touched again.

Source cannot die as it can only transform, and it can only create. Source is sacred and thus mysterious, and as we all know, anything truly sacred is beyond word-connected thought and thus beyond a thought-form understanding. Thus, sacred texts will always fail to encompass The All and usually lead to extremism and chaos. Nothing created by

Source can die. Everything merely transforms—just like Source—for everything is in Source's image, The All. Source can be glimpsed within the space between atoms and molecules because it not only forms the space, it is the space, the vibration, and the attraction. Yet even this is not The All of Source; it is only an observable aspect of Source for those who pay attention.

Sometimes the creative force of Source looks like destruction to earthbound minds, but this is only because Source is not bound by space or time. Vibrational rates are a manifestation of Source, but they are not Source. Some call Source the "Void," and this symbol-creation works for them. For everything indeed comes from the Void and returns to the Void, and The All has already been created only to cycle and be re-created endlessly within endless forms. This is the sacred mystery of how Source first created the Sacred Mother of our Sacred Mother, and how the Earthtribe was first created. From Source alone came The All, thus Source is The All. Though this is unknowable, I still call Source "Great-Grandmother." Many within the Earthtribe do as well. We seem to like this designation because it soothes a temporarily earthbound mind.

Source cares not about race, wealth, national or religious pride, sports heroes, actresses, actors, singers, talk show hosts, war, social position, belief, or lack of belief. This is because it creates only free will, and those things are all created in turn by the expressions that were first created by Source. Source just is and can be experienced but never explained, controlled, understood, or codified. We who are created by Source have created time in our own image. Using this beautiful and practical illusion, we date the universe as having been brought into being by Source 13.7 billion years ago.

Source, however, is beyond time. We carefully ignore this fact, though, because this is also soothing to a temporarily earthbound mind. Since we are the creators of time as we understand it, we can count these numbers as being correct or incorrect because we also created the numbers, even though numbers and time cannot contain or explain Source. As beings from Source, we are also creators, and thus, we can create a Heaven or a Hell or anything in between. We can also create realities beyond Heaven or Hell, but many of us do not realize this yet. We will. Some have named Source "The Big Bang," but this is only an emanation from the Void and thus cannot be Source—it is only an example of something coming into being from the Void and something that will eventually return to the Void. Something of Source and not actually Source. It is simply The Heartbeat of Source. A limitless heartbeat that will continue creating endlessly. We experience the pause between beats and then reason the pause to be the totality of existence when it is simply something coming into being. This is the sacred truth of Being-Becoming that few can understand, much less translate from the original Sanskrit.

We, born from the Earth Mother that our Primordial Mother Source first created and gave birth to— only one of innumerable Mothers within uncountable multiverses—thus, in turn, creating Her, the source of Us, seek always to understand and even (rather stupidly) to interpret, comprehend, and master Source. This is because we can sense the celestial knowledge within Source, even if we cannot comprehend it. Since Source exists in a realm far beyond word-connected thought, the word "master" means nothing to Source and is only a creation from the many new creators that Source brings forth via the Void. This is all a fool's errand, but a noble enterprise within our current, collective evolution and transformational process.

We only need to experience Source and with that experience will come enough understanding. However, we do not, as a species, quite understand all this yet. We will. For one day we will transform. One day we will realize that we are only one tribe, the Earthtribe and that it is impossible to be separate from our collective Source. We are One. We are The All. We are Source, and She is Us for we all were born from the same Source. There is no duality, no separation from Source or from each other. We are Earthtribe, Planetary Citizens, but also Universal Citizens and Multiversal Citizens. We are made of everything that the uncountable galaxies are constructed of. All else that contradicts this self-evident truth must one day be seen for what it is, Maya/illusion. An illusion that is self-perpetrated for we create it all. If you think we are separate, remember Fukashima, and remember the Pacific Ocean. It is all transforming before your eyes. We are one planet, one people, and there is no backyard. Anywhere.

Source gave our universe what it needed to create for this is what Source always does. Using created thought forms, we have named the unnameable gifts that Source has continually bestowed upon us. Strong and weak nuclear forces, gravitational pull, the elemental table, electromagnetic forces—these were all created from the dust left over by exploding stars. Using our word-connected thought-form that created numbers, we estimate the Earth Mother to have begun cooling around 4.6 billion years ago, and all reckoned in our self-created time—even though we know time has no actual reckoning. We have proven this, yet at this time, we cannot overcome our self-imposed limitations in order to transcend our current self-imposed, duality-driven developmental level.

Gasses came into being for they were needed in order to create Her. Hydrogen, helium, carbon dioxide, water vapor, ammonia, and oxygen all came from Source, and we in turn created what we needed to understand as best we could these precious gifts from Source in our current transformation. (We have, however, missed the sacred mystery in so doing.) Gravitational pull brought into being stars, planets, and their orbiting moons, meteors, comets, asteroids, and all forms needed for life to begin within. The many creations from Source coalesced together to create their own creations in turn, for this is the sacred nature, miracle, and true mystery of Source. The essence of the creator is always found within all that is created, this is why it is easy to know the deception of duality once you experience Source. What is within is also without. That which is above is also below.

Sometimes that which seems evil is good, and that which seems good is evil. Discernment helps the earthbound mind when it comes to duality.

The Primordial Mother of the Earthtribe Mother (Source's daughter, one of uncountable daughters within uncountable multiverses) obviously loved water because she was originally covered in it. We, the children of her child, in turn, are made from it. Our tears remind us of Her as they still carry the primordial salts of her being. We are truly stardust water beings just like her, and we are constructed of all that is Her. This is the nature of Source. This is the nature of The All. This is also unknowable.

About 3.5 billion years ago, calculated using our thought-form symbols that meant nothing during that transformation because we had not created time yet, Primordial Earth Mother (Grandmother) brought forth her first young. She began creating as she in turn was created, always following the prime directive of Source as all must do even when they refuse to do so. For even in refusing to follow Source, one still does the will of Source, for The All works to the benefit of Source regardless. This is unstoppable because Source always is, always does, and can never do anything other than create that which creates. These single-celled organisms led to multicelled organisms, and about 750 million years ago, plants and animals began to come into being. True growth happens during transformation and things always grow more complex as they transform.

Again, time meant nothing 750 million years ago because we were not there yet to create time in our own image and thus install limits upon existence. Source is beyond time always and thus acts outside of time always and as such is limitless. Though we use mental constructs to glimpse Source we do not define Source for our mental constructs cannot yet do this. The All will simply not fit within our mental and psychological creations even though they are of The All. Within the inherent limitations of the symbolic thought form we call language, many have become temporarily lost and thus conclude that there is no free will. This is incorrect. Source encompasses more than can be understood within a symbolic thought-form. That which leads to thought leads to freedom, but that which leads to thought can also lead to thought forms that lead, in turn, to chains of the mental, spiritual, and physical variety. That which leads to Source will lead one beyond word-connected thought and once therein, one finds answers and acceptance. Since this process is unknowable, it remains a mystery to many, though secretly known by some. Usually the innocent, for they are not fond of duality and do not like to dwell within the socially/economically/theoretically/racially/ and falsely created two camp continuums of "them" and "us." The innocent are born knowing that there is no "them" and there is no "us"—there is only The All.

About 150,000 years ago our Mother was born from Her Mother, Earth. Our collective Mother knew nothing of time for time was not yet invented and thus meant nothing.

She knew of cycles: sun cycles, moon cycles, her sacred cycles, and the cycles of plants and animals, though the concept of "animal" was not yet in vogue. One of Mother's children, Rebecca Cann, being a creator herself and thus creating in turn, in her Earth Mother's image, chose to devote herself to science, the study of DNA, and the pursuit of knowledge. For this is what those who create do—they always pursue knowledge. They seek the fountainhead of Source because this is a prime directive if you listen.

She and others listened because they knew that listening facilitates learning. This Earth Sister and her Earth Brother, Allen Wilson, mapped DNA and used matrichronology to show that all human lines trace back to the ovaries of a single Mother and were brought forth by Earth Mother around 150,000 years ago. Using our newly created symbol-language, we have named the place of Her birth "Africa." We are Her children. Our Father was called "Adamu" by some, meaning "Son of the Red Mother Earth." Other researchers are tracing his trail even as I write this. The DNA markers of our primordial parents are carried within our sacred and magical bloodlines. Our very lifeblood sings this ancient and truly magical song of creation. We are One People. We are one tribe. We are Earthtribe. And we have forgotten this. We must remember because it is this sacred truth that can save us all.

Our Earth Sister Rebecca Cann collected DNA from other Sisters: Sisters from Asia, Europe, the South Pacific, and Americans of African descent. Her Earth Brother in science, Mark Stoneking, collected DNA from other Earth Sisters, including aboriginal Australians and New Guineans. They published their results in the magazine *Nature*, and in doing so, proved that we are all children of the Earthtribe—we are all related. We all come from Our Mother, the collective Mother. The One. She was a child of Mother Earth, our Grandmother, created in turn from Source, our Great-Grandmother, and We are Her and She is Us because, again, it is impossible to be separate from Source. We are One People. The People of Earth. We are a planetary tribe. The Earth is our collective home. We are Earthtribe. Look around and see Source in everyone and know that we must cease killing and hating one another. When we kill each other, we truly murder our own brothers and sisters. When we hate each other, we hate our own family, our own tribe, our own mother, our own father.

The incarceration process causes you to separate from other people based on skin color, ethnicity, and location. You become numb in some areas of your consciousness. You soon forget the simple things you used to enjoy as a child. You forget that babies are never born racist. You may reminisce sometimes about "free person" activities such as driving a car, or going to a restaurant, but over time, the mind-numbing monotony and freedom from choice inherent within the prison routine will have influenced the way you think. After a few years of prison life, you will gladly accept the same segregated life you have behind bars. You will also accept the destructive idea of "them" versus "us." You will, in effect, be eating garbage and calling it ice cream. This happened over time. Slowly you began to accept things as they were, dreaming about what might be later and living in the future. A future that had not manifested yet. A future unlikely to manifest due to your current poor choices. What would have been a nightmare as a free person became the daily grind as an inmate. You became a prisoner psychologically and thus you began to act like a prisoner socially.

The segregation process inherent in prison will not serve you well in the free world.

Seeing this process can begin growth in a new direction.

I am asking you to remember your childhood. Do not focus on what you did not have or who was mean to you. I want something different from you. Were there things you loved to do? Were there things you wanted to do but were not able to do? If you could do them today, would you? When you played, what were your innermost dreams? What did you daydream about? What did you want to become? Who did you want to be? Did you have heroes? Who were they? Why were they heroes to you? I am asking you to think deeply and fearlessly about these things. The dreams of childhood that whispered to your heart.

Remember what you loved before you were a prisoner.

Can you remember a time when you could enjoy yourself without using drugs or alcohol? Over time, people involved in criminal and addictive lifestyles develop criminal and addictive thinking patterns. These thinking patterns are reinforced by the social interactions and the company we keep. Culture matters. In recovery, we call this kind of enmeshment in a toxic lifestyle "The Culture of Addiction." If you are doing life on the installment plan, you are enmeshed in the toxic culture of criminality. Usually, these cultures are combined because drug culture cannot exist without crime, and criminal culture needs the drug culture for its "profit margin."

Pleasures once enjoyed without drugs become paired with drugs. Over time the drug use becomes the pleasure. Then it makes you a slave as it hijacks your brain. Pizza tastes better after a joint, driving, dancing, and playing pool all go better with tobacco, cocaine, alcohol, or meth. Your brain is an expert at making connections, and the more those connections are used, the stronger they become. You attract into your life what you think about. The basic, simple pleasures are still there for you if you choose to seek out those pleasures. You originally enjoyed those activities without drugs. You also have the power to seek out new pleasures and do the things you only dreamed about as a child. You have the power to create new connections. New life experiences become new connections. New connections become new pathways.

You have the power to choose. Choose wisely.

Throughout all this time you have had choices. Many more choices are in store for you. The choices will never stop. Lessons will continue until they are learned.

Many former inmates give up on ever belonging in the "free world" again because they believe they will never "fit in" or be accepted. They feel that it just involves too much work to overcome a felony conviction. While it is true that creating a new life from the ashes of an old way of being in the world does require hard work and dedication, it is not an impossible task. If you think of recreating yourself as hard and almost impossible work, you will lose the benefits inherent within the process of recreating yourself. By recreating yourself, you will gain social abilities that you never dreamed possible. It all starts with empathy, but more on that later. The criminal justice system can be predatory and unforgiving, but it can be dealt with in a healthy manner. You will probably get tired of the process of recreating yourself and want to give up. Do not give anyone that satisfaction. You deserve your best effort. If you change the way you think about rehabilitation—and yourself in the process—you are more likely to stick with probation/parole and gain an important personal victory over whatever probation/parole challenges you struggle with.

The reality of parole is that it will challenge you. It will sometimes add positive stress to your life, and it can also add negative stress. Positive stress adds to your well-being. Taking a jujitsu class or enrolling in a gym are forms of positive stress. Positive stress makes you stronger and adds to your quality of life. Positive stress can become a beautiful process of self-discovery. To become independent of the criminal justice system, you will have to develop empathy for yourself and others, even others with a different skin tone. Even those who are different culturally. True self-empathy means getting to know yourself and creating a positive, healthy, and kind relationship with yourself. This process will translate to other people as well. Parole survival challenges give you a chance to explore your mind and gain a better understanding of how you relate to the world in general, and people in particular. Empathy is powerful because it works. Empathy will help you survive because it requires radical self-honesty. When you commit to being honest about your own motivations, you will gain insight into why you did things in the past and why you do some things presently. You will also learn to suspend judgment of others based on lifestyle, culture, and skin tone. Developing empathy for yourself can be the catalyst for some very powerful changes that you may need to make in your current life. The first step to personal growth is empathy for yourself because it leads to empathy for others.

The fact is that you are on parole or probation, and that means supervision by a criminal justice employee. You have to be with yourself every twenty-four-hour cycle until you die. During your life sentence on the third planet from the sun, you are the only person that you can never lose or leave. You are stuck with yourself. You are also stuck with the other Homo sapiens that share the planet with you. You are a product of your society, culture, and upbringing. Since this is the reality on planet earth, why not do everything in your power to get to know yourself better? When you are honest about your past and present, you can learn to accept yourself and find internal peace. Are you willing to learn how to love yourself? (Be careful, this process will cause you to gain empathy for others!) You must believe and understand that you are worthy of the time and effort required to heal your relationship with yourself and society. This healing is necessary so that you can create a new life, free of supervision by others. Since you are the one person creating your thoughts, the thoughts that drive you every day, why not master them? You have no choice other than to be with yourself anyway, so why not learn to be your own best friend?

I am just a good, old-fashioned drug counselor. When I say that recovery is a beautiful process of self-discovery, this is meaningful for people on parole. Most people assume that a successful recovery is simply about abstinence from The Big Six: drugs, alcohol, gambling, sex, pornography, or binge eating. You ended up on parole due to a dysfunctional relationship with accepted societal behavior. And, just like The Big Six give fellow Homo sapiens some temporary pleasure and relief, you did things that gave you pleasure, excitement, and relief. Once on parole, it can seem like an unattainable challenge when you have to give up an old way of being in the world.

Survival on parole, just like recovery, is all about learning a new way to live again. You were enmeshed in a culture of criminality. Getting out of that culture will be a process that requires effort. It will require more than just talking about leaving it or dreaming about it. Your old way of life must become invalidated by a new way of life. This process will be all about changing your old thinking patterns. It will involve learning new thinking patterns that will help create new behaviors. The fact is cold and hard: you have to give up your former way of life. This is a good thing because your old way of thinking led to imprisonment. It was not working for you anyway, and neither was the culture of criminality. You are engaged in recovery now—recovering your free life, unencumbered by supervision. A new life that offers the only true freedom, the freedom to embrace your highest good. The culture of criminality will always keep you in bondage even if you successfully complete parole. By staying honest with yourself as you go through the life recovery process, you will learn to know and accept the real you. Only then can you learn to love and appreciate who you truly are. This process will begin with empathy, and it will teach you to love, like, and accept other humans. This will become a powerful and transformative blessing. A gift that keeps on giving.

Make a strong commitment that you will be successful on parole. While parole/probation may not be an easy or painless process, it is worth your highest effort because YOU are worth it! You have the right to experience life free of overt supervision. A life guided by right action and personal fulfillment. Make the commitment that you are going to complete your term of supervision even if you think it is "not worth it." Your old way of life will become invalidated by new growth. This is an inescapable fact.

Your goals in life are worth working for. Stop looking at parole/probation as a difficult task that must be endured. When you see this new set of experiences as a healthy challenge and a good investment of time and energy, the journey will become much more positive and fulfilling. It is a timeless truth that your thoughts change your perspective.

You do not need permission from anyone to think. However, you may need your own permission to think.

You can find healing. You can find happiness. You can no longer be dependent upon the opinions of other people. You can find fun again. You can live with no expectations of others and no need to seek their approval. You have the power to let go of anger, fear, and past resentments. You have the power to find a pastime that will help you stay in the present moment. It may be a gym, a class, or a hobby like hiking, art, or bike riding—whatever it is, it is out there for you to find. When you find it, and you will, the result will be that you become stronger in other areas of your life that benefit from staying in the moment. (Like personal interactions with society in general, and with people in particular.) Your task is to find your pastime. Find the activity that reinforces your present moment focus skills. Find the activity that you can lose yourself in. Once you accomplish this, your life will begin to change for the better. The activity does not have to be physical either. It can be reading, writing, art, or writing poetry—whatever you choose to allow into your awareness. Regardless, it will all begin with personal empathy.

You have the power to create new connections. New life experiences become new connections. New connections become new pathways.

Learn to choose what you love to do, no matter what other people think. Listen to the whisperings of your heart. You must learn to recover your humanity for it is the source of our passion and inspiration. We work as humans to pay bills and to live in the world, but we dance, sing, pursue photography, write poetry and music, explore nature, and seek expression in fun and in hobbies because we are human. These things we love to do are direct messages from our subconscious, guiding us to a greater purpose. Guiding us to happiness, leading us to the truth of our being, leading us to real freedom. Consider the positive possibilities.

"If life is not as you choose, make new choices regarding your life."
—Dante Kun

Let's explore empathy and why it is important. Being human requires empathy and compassion. Being successful requires empathy and compassion also. What is empathy?

Empathy is the innate human capacity to understand or feel what another person is experiencing regardless of their lifestyle choice, spiritual beliefs, skin tone, or culture. It is being able to understand another person's predicament or frame of reference. Empathy is the human ability to place oneself in another's position. This is seen as weak in the segregated world of prison. But in the free world, the exact opposite is true. Empathy and compassion are strengths. Empathy and compassion unite the Earthtribe.

What is compassion? Compassion is linked to empathy. Compassion is both a feeling and an action. Compassion is the ability to feel deep sympathy and sorrow for another person who is suffering, along with a strong desire to alleviate the suffering through direct action. This ability has helped the human race survive ancient environmental challenges like saber-toothed tigers, woolly mammoths, and short-faced bears. If you don't know what a short-faced bear is, look it up. This ancient creature makes a grizzly bear look anemic. Our ancestors faced them. Our ancestors overcame them.

Inside the segregated world of prison, you learned to suppress empathy and compassion for those who did not share your skin tone or culture. This was necessary for survival within the manufactured racist construct of prison. You did not dare to risk being seen as weak. A prisoner in my conflict resolution class at Pelican Bay State Prison once announced, "No bleeding in the shark tank." That was an accurate statement about interpersonal communication at Pelican Bay. In the free world, empathy and compassion are survival skills. They are powerful strengths that are force multipliers. You are alive because of empathy and compassion. You are the result of the strong survival skills of your ancestors. Modern humans have been alive on Earth for 150,000 to 180,000 years depending on which expert you listen to. You have a powerful lineage behind you. We know this is true because you are here. Your ancestors not only produced offspring, they also produced offspring that survived. You have an ancestral line that reaches back into ancient, primordial, and very difficult times. You come from a long line of survivors. They faced challenges you can only dream about. Those dreams would be nightmares.

Most people focus on how harsh life was in ancient times, and how "survival of the fittest" (usually understood as who is the most violent) ensures that a person will survive. Prison life supports this idea. I say that our survival for thousands of years was also due in large part to humans being loyal, kind, cooperative, and supportive of each other. Our abilities to honor agreements and tribal rules made us stronger than the competition. Our young are born helpless and depend on interactions with older, more experienced people to hand down knowledge and thus improve each generation. Family and cultural ties matter. Compassion and empathy are the bonds of family, tribe, and culture. Your ancient ancestors survived not just by being violent, they also had compassion and empathy for their people. Without empathy and compassion driving ancient humans to help one another, the species of Homo sapiens would not have lasted long against ancient environmental challenges. The ability to feel empathy benefits all social relationships between humans.

Why you need to cultivate and develop empathy and co-occurring compassion.

Empathy will enable you to become a better friend, coworker, partner, and overall better human being. People will like that quality in you and respond well to it. Empathy will help you understand the needs of your fellow human beings that you interact with each day. This, in turn, will benefit your relationships with those people. The magic of cultivating empathy is that you will treat people how you want to be treated because you will understand what they need from you. This is the golden rule of life. The expression of empathy in the free world is never a mistake.

You will gain insight by cultivating empathy with others. You will gain insight into how other people feel as well as the personal insight that will strengthen your awareness of how you affect others. Your social, personal, and professional relationships will improve as a direct result of your empathy-driven insights. When you gain the ability to truly understand another person's position and viewpoint, you have gained a powerful survival tool in the free world. You will have the superpower of understanding and evaluating how your actions, behavior, and words affect the people in your life. Your family, friends, coworkers, employers—everybody. You will understand the true influence you have when communicating with people. You will overcome the fear-based and destructive communication you used in prison.

Cultivating empathy with your fellow human beings will improve your ability to understand non-verbal cues such as facial expressions, body language, and blended micro-expressions. In prison, your intuition became fine-tuned to anticipate violence. In the free world, that can be useful in some situations. It is also important to understand unspoken communication that involves kindness, compassion, and awareness of other people's vulnerabilities, feelings, and challenges. The more you learn to practice empathy, the better you will interact with fellow humans in the work environment, in social spaces, and at home.

You will be an asset at work and not a liability. Your family and social interactions will improve. Empathy will improve your ability to anticipate the challenges and needs of your family, friends, coworkers, and customers. Cultivating empathy will strengthen your ability to know the challenges that other people face. You will gain a better understanding of your friends, coworkers, and family. As a result of heightened empathic abilities, you will become a more effective communicator in social, work, and family settings.

Your ability to navigate conflict without violence will improve as a result of your embracing empathy in daily life. Far from becoming weak, you only gain more internal strength when you cultivate empathy. Your relationships, social, professional, family, and personal, will all improve by understanding the "other side" in conflict situations.

Misunderstandings become opportunities to understand each other rather than devolving into violence and insanity. Empathy helps reason rule the day rather than anger. Empathy helps both sides realize that conflict can lead to cooperation.

Empathy will help you understand that all human behavior is motivated by something. You will better understand the motivation that drives most fellow humans regardless of their race or culture. By cultivating empathy, you will be able to accurately predict the actions and reactions of your fellow humans. Empathy is a strength, never a weakness. Your interaction with humanity will improve along with your life experiences as a direct result of developing a stronger sense of empathy and compassion.

Your interpersonal focus will improve with empathy. As you gain skill and focus in recognizing the motivations driving human behavior, your relationships will improve. Your interactions with family, friends, and coworkers, will be guided by a new and powerful internal understanding on your part. Your communication will become solid, assertive, and compelling rather than aggressive. Through empathy, you will gain the ability to better predict the behavior (actions and reactions) of others.

The cultivation of empathy multiplies the strength of your interpersonal communication. The golden rule "Do unto others as you would have them do unto you" (Matt. 7:12) is a gift that keeps on giving. It is the cornerstone of empathy and compassion. You can inspire other people when you understand how they want to be treated. The golden rule will help you motivate others to achieve positive goals in life, work, and relationships because empathy is a powerful motivator. Empathy and compassion inspire humanity to achieve greatness. You will become an inspiration to others, and that is never a bad thing.

When you embrace empathy, you can help others understand your position. This is because you understand their position better. Empathy is an effective and powerful communication tool. People tend to listen to you when you are a good listener in return. People also admire a responsible human being, and someone who has demonstrated they are a caring person. They are more likely to understand your position if they are willing to listen to you. Empathy is a magnet that attracts listeners.

Empathy will help you connect with people better because you will gain heightened insight into their concerns, challenges, issues, and viewpoints. Instead of only focusing on your own challenges or perspective, empathy is the superpower that will help you see the underlying concepts that connect individual perspectives.

Empathy will help you be a better communicator. Using empathy in communication will help you understand people on a much more intense level. You will be a more efficient worker, and you will naturally help inspire people to do and be better. Your relationships will improve when you bring empathy to the table. The best of friends, spouses, and leaders are all compassionate and caring.

Empathic skills are the ones you can develop with practice. Prison may have conditioned you to curb empathy, but the free world is not prison. People communicate differently in the free world. Here are some ways to develop healthy levels of empathy that will lead to active compassion.

Learn some new skills and have fun doing it. You are not in prison anymore. Take a jujitsu class or enroll in a class at the local college. Practice your guitar skills or join a drumming class. Get out of your comfort zone and embrace life. Take a cooking class and learn about different cultural foods. You know how to survive in prison because you know how people survive in prison. Now is your time to learn how the free world operates. Take a walking tour of your neighborhood. Go to a local park, try new foods at new restaurants you never thought of going to. Try food from other parts of our culturally rich planet. Learn a foreign language. Ride a mountain bike on a trail even if you have to drive to get there. Join a dance class and make new friends. Trying new things, learning new skills, and meeting new people will help you develop social flexibility. This process will help you develop empathy. You already know to interact with inmates, so now learn how to interact with people who have never been inmates. Welcome yourself into the free world. Realize that you have potential teachers all around you. The free world has many people from whom you can learn and grow. A casual coffee shop conversation might expose you to a new viewpoint or a unique perspective. Open yourself up and meet people with an attitude of learning something new. It can be about yourself or about them. No matter how the message is presented to you, the message can deliver insight if you listen to it. The more you are able to focus on others, the better you listen instead of talk, the greater your ability to understand unique viewpoints, cultures, values, history, and individual perspectives will expand.

Don't allow defensive, fear-based thinking to crush authentic communication and healthy dialogue. Defensive, segregated thinking is a prison skill. Open-minded, inclusive thinking is a free-world skill. The free world is filled with people from all over the planet. In prison, you were manipulated to only associate with "your kind." You can do that in the free world, too, but you would be missing out on new experiences. I'm not saying to just blindly trust everyone. You must use reasonable caution. I am saying that it is not wise to just write everyone off and be an island unto yourself. Humans are social, so get social. Learning about different ideas, lifestyles, cultures, and customs will develop your social perspective. This is a good thing, and it only makes you stronger. It can sometimes be a struggle but being open to other people's ideas and views on politics, culture, customs, and social morals only increase your empathic abilities. Learning to respect other views and gaining cultural empathy only makes you a better communicator.

Good listeners are good communicators. Stay relaxed but alert and make eye contact when appropriate. Try to listen without judging the person. Realize that the conversation is about an exchange of ideas and views. It is not about "winning" or making a point. You are no longer in prison, so it is OK to listen and allow a conversation to proceed freely rather than controlling it.

Embrace the attitude of gratitude. Be grateful for being alive, for healthy change, for new choices, for new people, and for new experiences. When you show others appreciation for kindness, it opens the way for people to show you appreciation. Thank people you meet—bus drivers, taxi drivers, waitresses, waiters, store clerks, and people at work. Thank them for what they do and what you learn from them. They might not even know they taught you anything. You might make their day. Practicing empathy is like working out. The more you practice, the stronger and better you become.

I challenge you to begin the path toward personal and spiritual bliss. I challenge you to begin doing what you love and loving what you do. I want you to begin exercising your freedom of choice muscle. Doing this will involve your fellow Homo sapiens. It will involve healthy communication. In the process, you will gain empathic skills. You are up to the task; I have no doubt about it. You survived prison, and it is time to survive and thrive while on parole. I want you to find those things you loved to do or think you might love to do. Did you ever want to surf or skydive? Hike, camp, ride a mountain bike? Write a book? Learn a foreign language? Do you love working out? What about becoming a fitness trainer and leading others toward a healthy lifestyle? Do you enjoy reading, swimming, and espresso coffee? When you leave any prison behind, you have a golden opportunity to choose again, regardless of whether that prison was made of stone and steel or if that prison was a mental construct created by you and others around you.

You had *freedom from choice* in prison, you have *freedom of choice* now. What will you do?

You have the freedom to create a new life, a new reality. You can get a job, you can work two jobs, you have that choice. In prison, you made maybe twenty-five cents per hour (or, in some prisons, even less). You will make a lot more than that in the free world. You can work at night, go to school during the day, or do the reverse. You can find something that creates passion in your life and makes you feel inspired. You can follow that inspiration. You can choose again. You can also choose to take the path to destruction and do a life sentence on the installment plan. Or worse. Personal choice is powerful. You can choose to stay within abusive, toxic relationships. You can choose to abuse drugs and alcohol, stay enmeshed in the culture of addiction and/or criminality and repeat the same old dysfunctional behaviors that lead to prison. You are free to ignore treatment options. You can choose to stay angry and allow guilt, anger, and regret to manage your life for you. You can choose to take the path right back to prison, violate parole or probation, and return to life as a prisoner. You can be "empathy free" and be the "tough guy." You can go right back to *freedom from choice* and make that your comfort zone.

It is your choice, and it's all up to you.

I challenge you to create a list. This will be the only exercise for this chapter. It will be harder than it seems. I want you to write down one hundred things you would like to experience. It does not matter if you have done some of these things, or if they are things you only dreamed of doing. They must be legal and fun. They can be dreams of childhood or dreams and desires you had in prison. As you create this list, I challenge you to be, as Henry David Thoreau put it, "independent of the good opinion of others." What you put on your list can be expensive, free, or inexpensive. I have only one major requirement, and that is to allow your heart to lead you.

The past is dead; you are not your past. The future has not yet happened. You have only the present moment, from moment to moment, and your choices within each moment will become your future. Seeing this process can begin growth in a new direction. Consider the positive possibilities. You had freedom from choice in prison, you have freedom of choice now. What will you do?

The List Exercise

I have included my current list as an example. This is not my first list. I have completed some things on my list and am in the process of completing others. As you go through the journey of life and encounter lessons, you will make choices. Out of those choices, you will change and grow. Your list will change and grow right along with you. As you experience life events, things that were once important to you may lose importance. Other desires that were trivial or nonexistent may come to the forefront and become important. The foremost idea behind this exercise is that you choose these desires. You practice making healthy, positive choices.

Something that may seem small and insignificant today may pull at your heartstrings years from now.

It is important to honor desire because desire is your inner self guiding you. It is in knowing the importance of the small things that we gain an appreciation for the larger things in life that come our way. This is not a trivial exercise. I consider it one of the most important exercises in this workbook. If you cannot make life-affirming choices, you are emotionally crippled. There is nothing "funny" about this exercise. Your inability to make healthy, positive, life-affirming choices landed you in prison. By your very own choices, you ended up with the boot of the law on your neck. You were so incapable of making healthy choices that you put yourself in a situation where others made your choices for you. Your family suffered with you. This list is no joke when done honestly. It is a road map created entirely by your heart and it will guide you to freedom.

If you talk more than you listen. If you "stay ready so you don't have to get ready." If it's always "go time" for you. If you cannot control your impulses. If you are always right and everyone else is always wrong, your ego is in charge and you are on your way back to prison. You cannot handle freedom of choice.

This exercise is about *freedom of choice*, not *freedom from choice*. This exercise is about you controlling your brain, your body's biological computer, and not allowing your computer to control you. Now is not the time to lie to yourself about your tactical situation. Your life and many possible choices are governed by a judge, a probation officer, and any police officer who decides to randomly speak with you. You are on a leash that is being controlled by the criminal justice system. You are not free yet; you are an inmate on probation or parole. Your life choices are critical because they will determine your future. Begin to choose wisely and make your first list. Take your first real steps toward true and lasting freedom. Real freedom. You have this present moment to make a map, so allow the whisperings of your heart to make a good one. Do not simply copy my list items unless there is something on it you like.

There is no magic way to earn self-esteem. There is only one true way to gain it. That way is by setting goals and accomplishing those goals.

1. Go hiking.
2. Go bowling.
3. Learn to write better Haiku.
4. Finish my book of poetry.
5. Eat at Snow City Café.
6. Update my Facebook status (which I never seem to do).
7. Climb stairs.
8. Go to the Sea Life Center in Homer.
9. Go camping.
10. Learn how to recognize even more thinking errors.
11. Play darts.
12. Hike Table Mountain.
13. Go to Kaladi Brothers coffee and just hang out with my laptop.
14. Go to a bookstore.
15. Go to Organic Oasis.
16. Visit Talkeetna more often.
17. Write more poetry.
18. Take another course on logic.
19. Go to a spoken word event.
20. Speak at a spoken word event.
21. Practice archery.
22. Visit Seattle.
23. Spoil my grandson.

24. Spoil my granddaughter.
25. Listen to Mozart.
26. Rent a DVD.
27. Ride a fat tire bike.
28. Visit Eklutna lake.
29. Meditate.
30. Build a bonfire on the beach.
31. Get better at Spanish.
32. Write in my journal more often.
33. Bodyboard at Crescent Beach again.
34. Practice logic.
35. Listen to Beethoven.

> "Our job is to straighten out our own lives."
> —Joseph Campbell

36. Buy some music.
37. Take my wife on a road trip.
38. Write a chapter outline.
39. Go to a play.
40. Volunteer.
41. Subscribe to an online magazine I really like.
42. Start a blog.
43. Build a driftwood house on the beach.
44. Watch a sunset.
45. Take more pictures.
46. Cruise around in my truck drinking Kaladi Brothers coffee and listening to music.
47. Take a hike around a new lake.
48. Barbecue.
49. Call my mom.
50. Picnic and grill at Finger Lake.
51. Camp at Finger Lake.
52. Take pictures at Finger Lake.
53. Take pictures of Salmon.
54. Take pictures of what beavers do to trees.
55. Paint on a canvas.
56. Take pictures of Mirror Lake.
57. Laze around on my day off drinking coffee and reading the Sunday paper.

58. Post pictures on Facebook.
59. Buy and use an underwater drone.
60. Take a pottery class.
61. Watch a self-hypnosis video.
62. Hike with a friend.
63. Work out on my heavy bag.
64. Get over my fear of flying drones because I'm afraid to crash.
65. Take a software class.
66. Drink a plant-based protein shake every day.
67. Visit the Funny River.
68. Plant a garden.
69. Visit Seward.
70. Listen to jazz.
71. Go on a road trip.
72. Visit Amsterdam.
73. Visit Hawaii.
74. Bodyboard South Beach.
75. Go to Marine World.
76. Go to a concert.
77. Hang a hammock at the beach and spend the night.
78. Cook salmon over a fire on the beach.
79. Eat at the Rain Forest café.
80. Spend the day in Berkeley.
81. Take a ride on the Alaska Railroad.
82. Paraglide.
83. Read about an ancient culture.
84. Bodyboard with my sons and my daughter.
85. Take pictures of moose.
86. Read the collected works of Poe.
87. Use a sauna.
88. Visit a game preserve.
89. Read more Stanislav Grof.
90. Visit Alyeska.
91. Explore the Kenai Peninsula.
92. Pick wild blueberries.
93. Build a home gym.
94. Watch my son drumming.
95. Go to the Arctic Man Festival.
96. Take my wife out to an early morning breakfast.

97. Listen to a lecture by Christopher Hitchens.
98. Watch a *Game of Thrones* marathon with friends.
99. Make soap with my wife.
100. Hike downtown Anchorage.

Learn to choose what you love to do, regardless of the opinions of others. Listen to the whisperings of your heart. The past is dead; you are not your past. The future has not yet happened. You have only the present moment, from moment to moment, and your choices within each moment will become your future. Seeing this process can begin growth in a new direction.

> "What you leave behind is not what is engraved in stone
> monuments, but what is woven into the lives of others."
> —Pericles

Now make your own list. This will be one of the best things you can do for yourself. Making this list will help you remember things you have long forgotten about or gave up ever doing. This list can rekindle hope and act as a road map to a better life. Do you want to go back to college or trade school? Put it on the list. List your long- and short-term goals. Start making wise choices. When you are done, post your list. On your wall, on your refrigerator, wherever—place it somewhere obvious so that you see it several times a day. Make it the first thing you see upon waking up and the last thing you see before bed.

Choose wisely.
You are not your past.
You are not your anger.
Consider the positive possibilities.

The only action you can take in the present moment is to accept the past and the lessons you have learned, then learn from those lessons and move on. Any other action allows the past to rule your present moment, and all you have is your present moment. Regret is a time bandit. Don't allow regret to rob you of your present moment in time.

Remember what you loved before you ever became a prisoner.

The past is dead; you are not your past. The future has not yet happened. You have only the present moment, from moment to moment, and your choices in each moment will become your future. If you talk more than you listen, if it's always "go time" for you, if you cannot control your impulses, if you are always right and everyone else is always wrong, your ego is in charge and you are on your way back to prison. You cannot handle freedom of choice. All this time, you have had choices. Many more choices are in store for you. The choices will never stop. Lessons will continue until they are learned. Einstein's definition of insanity is doing the same thing over and over while expecting a different result. Don't do that.

> "The first question that the priest and the Levite asked was: 'If I stop to help this man, what will happen to me?' But the good Samaritan [...] always reverses the question: 'If I do not stop to help this man, what will happen to him?'"
> —Dr. Martin Luther King, Jr.

Chapter Four Affirmation

1. *I am a present moment master, and my wise choices reflect this.*

Chapter Four Reading Assignment

Pick a book written by an author who is from a different culture or race and read it.

Suspend judgment and pay attention to any "segregated thinking" leftover from prison life. Look for similarities. (You will find them!)

"The DNA markers of our primordial parents are carried within our sacred and magical bloodlines. Our very lifeblood sings this ancient and truly magical song of creation. We are One People. We are one tribe. We are Earthtribe. And we have forgotten this. We must remember, for it is this sacred truth that can save us all."...Dante B. Kun

CHAPTER FIVE

Presenting Yourself to the World

You have experienced some life lessons due to unwise choices. You can accept these lessons thus learned and resolve to make healthy choices in the only place you can choose to do so: the present moment. You only have the present moment, from moment to moment, in which to make change and decisions. You cannot change the past. You are not yet in the future; you have only this moment. When you meet new people, you will have only that present moment in time to present yourself. Your choices in language, dress, speech, body language, tone of voice, and facial expression will convey an image. That image will be interpreted as "you" by the new people meeting you for the first time. Choose wisely when you present yourself (your SELF) to the world. You have only the present moment, so use that finite moment in time well.

In prison, inmates wear "masks" every day. Within prison walls, each person chooses to project an image of themselves to others around them. Prison guards do this, inmates do it, and wardens do it. There is a very basic, human reason for this behavior—fear. Deep down you were afraid that you were not smart enough, strong enough, aggressive enough, or clever enough to avoid being victimized in the world you had to inhabit each day. The prison staff were afraid of being "gassed," beaten, or stabbed. Inmates were afraid of being harmed by staff or other inmates. It was a true circle of fear, intimidation, manipulation, and hatred. So, for many people, survival in prison entailed projecting an image that others would fear or respect, or preferably both fear and respect. Inside prison, fear and respect are two great things that go great together. Within a free society, the two never go well together.

Fear can result in you being put right back inside a steel and cement cage. In prison, racism is encouraged by the incarceration process. By becoming an inmate, you are automatically put in a racial category, and your fellow inmates will demand racial solidarity and loyalty. If you are white, you must associate with whites. If you are Black, you ride with the Black population. Latinos only with Latinos. If you are not Black, White, or Latino, then you are an Other. Gangs are an even greater challenge regarding affiliation. Being human has nothing to do with any of it. There are gang affiliations that strengthen this enforced division even further regardless of shared culture. In prison, these personal image projections were a survival skill. This "skill" was reinforced daily with posturing, threats, tattoos, language, violence, and affiliations. Your biggest challenge in the free world will lie in how you present yourself to others.

> "Peace is not merely a distant goal that we seek, but
> a means by which we arrive at that goal."
> —Dr. Martin Luther King, Jr.

If you choose to present yourself to others in the free world while wearing your old, outdated prison/inmate mask, you put yourself at risk. The mask that served you well walking around a prison exercise yard will do you nothing good while walking around the mall. You will instantly be identified and categorized as an "undesirable element." You become an instant target for law enforcement, parole agents, and "concerned citizens." This old prison mask will alienate you from the mainstream and potential employers. You will be at risk because it is not safe to present yourself in society like an aggressive inmate with violence bubbling up just beneath the surface.

First, let's clear up some misconceptions about prison versus free world values. I am going to get real with you, and you won't like it. Inmates and prisoners are seen and perceived as helpless, immature, emotionally crippled people. Most free people do not respect ex-inmates. They may fear them, but they do not respect them, and fear can cost you a lot within a free society. A potential employer may worry that you might steal from him or fight on the job. In the free world, respect and self-esteem come to you the old-fashioned way: you set goals, and you accomplish those goals. The free world operates on different standards and ways of thinking than the criminal and addictive ways of thinking that you are used to.

People in the free world admire successful people, and they respect accomplishment. That's why the NHL, NBA, NFL, UFC, and professional boxing industries are billion-dollar enterprises. Free people admire the beauty and courage of one man facing another in a cage. They pay money to watch this courage. They admire and respect the sportsmanship of professional sports. Four gang members stabbing an unarmed person to death is not bravery in the free world. It is perceived as abject cowardice. Drive-by shootings and the shooters who perpetrate them are perceived as the lowest of the low. Killing an entire family over drugs is perceived as the act of a cowardly animal. Yes, they might fear it, but they loathe and are repulsed by such acts. Respect is never in that equation. Inmates, parolees, and people who are "still in the game" are seen as forty-something, perpetual felon, forever adolescent, idiots. No one wants anything to do with them. You may not like that situation, but I would be lying to you if I implied anything less.

In prison, the forty-something gang member, perpetual criminal, emotionally stunted, and violent person who was always posturing about "respect" was given respect. Never in the free world will anyone who acts like that person earn respect—ever. They will, however, "earn" their way right back into a cage where they belong. Prison is not the free world and cannot prepare you for the free world.

The mask you wore in prison—the one that helped keep you alive—can cause another arrest and put you right back in prison while you are on parole. Dump that mask. It is a survival situation.

Please remember the following from earlier in this book:

"If you are in prison, jail, or on probation or parole, the universe has put you on notice. You simply cannot continue the old way and not suffer. You cannot continue the old way and not have your family suffer along with you. Your old way of life has been invalidated by a demand for new growth, and the universe is demanding this new growth immediately. I suggest you listen."

Start thinking like a true survivor.

The only action you can take in the present moment is to accept the past, learn from those lessons, and move on. Any other action allows the past to rule your present moment, and all you have is this present moment. If you talk more than you listen, if it's always "go time" for you, if you cannot control your impulses, if you are always right and everyone else is always wrong, your ego is in charge and you are on your way back to prison. You cannot handle freedom of choice. All this time, you have had choices. Many more choices are in store for you. The choices will never stop. Lessons will continue until they are learned.

Your first serious free world challenge will be to reveal aspects of yourself (your SELF) rather than hide aspects of yourself behind a mask. You will have to learn how to do this in a socially acceptable way. In prison, you learned to repress emotions and express others. You learned to hide your feelings and display only those feelings that enhanced survival and decreased victimization. Sometimes you learned that making others into your victims served you better because it decreased your chances of being taken advantage of while incarcerated.

How do you misuse your brain? Your brain is a biological computer. You have an amygdala and a limbic system. You have a hypothalamus. They are awesome. Your amygdala has several important jobs. One of them is to remember everything painful and pleasurable you have ever experienced. It does this with amazing precision. The amygdala operates seven times faster than normal thought. Crazy fast. It works like this: You see someone on the prison yard who has "disrespected" you in the past. Your amygdala saw him seven times faster than your first conscious acknowledgment of his presence. Your limbic system ignites, and your hypothalamus begins pumping out proteins and peptides. These proteins and peptides go straight to your cells that have developed specific receptor sites for them to lock onto, much like keys in a lock. Suddenly, you become your emotions. Your biological computer is in charge, not you. Thus begins a chemical cascade like a domino effect. The first domino is pushed over by your biological computer, and the rest fall with no effort on your part. You become a willing participant in an exercise in stupidity, futility, and ignorance. The dance of the criminal begins anew.

Anger is a secondary emotion—always. You choose to be angry. Your response is all yours—always. You cannot control what others do and say in the moment, but you have total control over what you do and say within that one precious moment in time. If you "stay ready so you don't have to get ready," the only thing you are ready for is a cell.

The only challenge we face is the mastery of our thoughts.
How to use your brain:

>   Choose wisely.
>   You are not your past.
>   You are not your anger, your feelings, or your emotions.
>   Consider the positive possibilities.

Know that whenever you feel an emotion you are feeling the action of a protein or peptide released by your hypothalamus due to your amygdala and limbic system. Giving in to this emotion in a negative, destructive way is akin to allowing your laptop computer to dictate your life and your immediate actions. Only a fool would do that. Free people do not allow their biological computer to rule their actions. The most aware people think before they act regardless of their personal feelings at that moment. This is called impulse control, and it is a function of your frontal lobes.

You are in prison because you have impulse control challenges that inhibit clear thinking before you speak or act. If your motivation is always selfish, you will always fail to think things through. Thus you cannot foresee possible negative outcomes or possible positive alternatives.

(If you talk more than you listen, if it's always "go time" for you, if you cannot control your impulses, if you are always right and everyone else is always wrong, your ego is in charge and you are on your way back to prison. You cannot handle freedom of choice. All this time, you have had choices. Many more choices are in store for you. The choices will never stop. Lessons will continue until they are learned.)

It is very easy to tell if you are not in control of your biological computer. Everything's an argument. If you constantly show up late for your work assignment, mealtimes, parole/probation appointments, and basically anything the staff asks of you, you are not in control. If you are constantly "defending" yourself from staff and other inmates every day, then you are not in control. If you spend your day engaging in multiple, twenty-minute, ego-fueled arguments with everyone; if you find fault in everyone and everything; if anger, hatred, and resentment are the "fuel" in your gas tank, then your emotions are in total control.

When your emotions are in control, you have lost all control.

Addictive and criminal thinking is always self-centered, and that is why everyone else is wrong except you. This type of interaction with people in the free world will exhaust others mentally, and they will simply shun you. You will be denied opportunity, and you won't even know what the opportunity was in the first place. No one will reach out to you in friendship except for other damaged, emotionally stunted, codependent people. If you don't change this dynamic, you are just heading back into the cage. If you want to change other people's opinions, show them rather than tell them. To be an example requires choice—always.

Your past is only an ancient reflection of old choices invalidated by new growth within the present moment.

Probationers and parolees who fail to succeed and return to custody make one of two mistakes: they try to fool themselves, or they try to fool others. There are two survival guidelines you should aspire to follow in the free world environment. It will be challenging at first for you to make these guidelines a lifestyle habit. They will feel unsafe and uncomfortable for you after years of prison life. Do not expect perfection right away. The most important thing you can do is make a sincere effort to follow these guidelines every day.

1. *Do not try to fool yourself.*

In prison, you may have aspired to be the menacing, strong, sometimes silent, sometimes loud inmate who always followed the "convict code." You know how it worked; you were "noble" if you went to the hole for someone else's misdeeds. You had little mantras that infected your thinking every day like "Nobody talks, everybody walks," "Snitches get stitches," or "Stay ready so you don't have to get ready." This was the macho way of being in prison. Proper emotions to display were anger, humor, and deception, all with the goal of manipulation. It was beneficial to be a little unpredictable and to have people afraid of you. To walk that thin line between compliance with authority and noncompliant, manipulative aggression.

Instant personal retaliation insured no future personal violation.

To present yourself in any other mask was to be perceived as vulnerable and weak. To be vulnerable and weak in prison is like bleeding in a shark tank. This was the price of safety and "respect" in prison. This is not the reality of the free world. If you hang on to the past and insist on wearing your old, useless prison mask that displays you as a dangerous, sometimes menacingly silent, sometimes too loud, immature, and unpredictable person in the free world, you will spend a lot of time alone and miserable. When not being alone and miserable, you can count on attracting codependent, damaged people with criminal and addictive-thinking errors into your life. They will quickly lead you into chaos, stupidity, and ultimately jail.

You will stay enmeshed in the familiar culture of criminality and addiction. But don't worry, you can always blame "them" later and thus avoid holding yourself accountable for your choices. You are free to stay lost in the chaos you create by your choices. Living up to this macho prison stereotype will negatively impact an entirely new life that is always available to you in the free world. It can strangle friendships before they are fostered. It can stifle job interviews. It can close you off to better times and better people in your life. You will attract the negativity you project out into the world. It does not have to be like that.

The mask you wore in prison, the mask that helped keep you alive—this very mask can cause your re-arrest and put you right back in prison while you are on parole. Dump that mask. It is a survival situation.

2. *Do not try to fool everyone else.*

You really won't fool everyone forever, so why try in the first place? Avoid the embarrassment guaranteed to come your way and just be real with yourself and everyone else. In prison, you became conditioned to a lifestyle based on fooling others. You attempted to fool everyone, all the time. Guards, counselors, case managers, teachers, other cons, other gangs, everyone within your contained and confined universe. A toxic universe that only offered freedom from choice within unrivaled negativity and concrete/steel walls. Do not try to duplicate on parole what you did in prison. If you think it will work, just check the recidivism rate. No one fools everyone all the time. Trust me; you are not a novelty to your probation officer. You may have thought you were so "on point" fooling people. You were always right and everyone else was stupid, clueless, and always wrong. You were one superior, cage-dwelling human. Go ahead, fake your drug test and be "proud." Sell and use drugs on parole. Be the smartest idiot on the block. Parole is just a joke anyway, am I right?

In prison, you kept secrets over stupid and petty conflicts. You played mind games just for the fun and practice of playing them. You fooled others about weapons and contraband. You fooled people about your crime of commitment and your lifestyle outside of prison. Like almost all prisoners, you told the same old familiar stories while locked up. Before prison, you were well-off, had a nice house, a wonderful relationship with many "fine" partners, and—of course—several awesome custom cars. You were only in prison due to a snitch, a bad lawyer, dirty cops, crooked judges, or just bad luck. Oh, and my favorite, your parole agent was an "asshole." Everyone else was wrong, and you were the only one right. Amazing.

Everyone around you did the same thing, told similar stories, and you accepted the "norm" of prison life. Lying to anyone who would listen about almost everything in your past became your present moment. Lying about a hoped-for future that your present choices doomed you from ever manifesting became your reality. This life of lies and continual destructive choices became a habitual ritual that hardwired itself into your mind. You became "convict conditioned"—a "prison prodigy." Instant retaliation insured no future violation. No one would ever make you "wrong." If anyone challenged your lies, they were "disrespecting" you and it was "go time." Your role in your own self-deception and destruction was never something you considered because you could never be wrong. Your self-deception had to be maintained, even if it meant resorting to violence. Your ego was so close to your position that if your position fell, your ego went with it. You could never allow that to happen.

There is no magic way to earn self-esteem, and no person can just give it to you. There is only one true way to gain it: the old-fashioned way. You must set goals and accomplish those goals. You have had some life lessons due to unwise choices, accept the lessons learned, and resolve to make healthy choices in the only place you can choose to do so: the present moment. You only have the present moment, from moment to moment, in which to make change and decisions. You cannot change the past. You are not yet in the future. You have only this moment. When you meet new people, you will have only that present moment in time to present yourself. Your choices in language, speech, body language, tone of voice, dress, and facial expression will convey an image. That image will be interpreted as "you" by the new people meeting you for the first time. Choose wisely when you present yourself (your SELF) to the world. You have only the present moment, so use that precious moment in time well.

"If you hang on to the past and insist upon wearing your old, useless prison mask that displays you as a dangerous, sometimes menacingly silent, sometimes too loud, immature person in the free world, you will spend a lot of your time alone and miserable. When not being alone and miserable, you can count on attracting codependent, damaged people with criminal and addictive thinking errors into your life. They will quickly lead you into chaos, stupidity, and ultimately jail, or back to prison. But don't worry, you can always blame 'them' and stay lost in the chaos you create by your choices."

Choices are everywhere, and choices impact the future as well as the present. Allowing your ego to rule your choices will lead only to despair. Everyone else will be wrong, and you will always be right. You will win every battle and lose the ultimate war for your freedom. Even when you are free of the criminal justice system, you will be an inmate. You will think like an inmate and act like an inmate. You will eventually return to the place where inmates live out their lives. All of it will reflect your choices.

Expressing yourself well is a key survival tactic outside prison walls. Being assertive—not aggressive—is the norm for a free society. Aggressive, verbally assaultive, angry, manipulative, abusive people eventually wind up on law enforcement's radar because the free world is designed for them to be located and neutralized. After all, it is law enforcement's job to notice angry, aggressive, dysfunctional people. Eventually, these people end up living in a cage where they eat food prepared by other angry, aggressive, unhappy, dysfunctional people. They also regularly use the toilet two feet from their bunk.

Do not end up eating bad food and using the toilet two feet from your bunk in front of a beady-eyed, aggressive, manipulative, emotionally stunted cell "partner." Learn to be assertive and not aggressive. Unless you like that lifestyle of course—no judgment. *The past is dead; you are not your past. The future has not yet happened. You have only the present moment, from moment to moment, and your choices within each moment will become your future. Seeing this process can begin growth in a new direction.* Consider the positive possibilities. You had *freedom from choice* in prison, and you have *freedom of choice* now. What will you do?

Start with being polite. This is not a weakness. The Harvard of bodyguard schools, Executive Security International, offers a course on international relations and manners. Professionally trained bodyguards are dangerous people, but they are polite and calm. They use assertive speech but are never aggressive. They solve dangerous situations without violence about ninety-nine percent of the time. When I went through the course, my instructors drilled an important mantra into my consciousness: "If you have to use violence, you did something wrong." Aggressive speech is violent speech. It sets the tone for no other course of action other than violent escalation.

Practice being polite every day. Smile at people. Say thank you to the person who rings up your groceries at the grocery store. Look people in the eye and be pleasant.

Practice being non-confrontational. Use your "I statements." "I see that you are stressed." "I feel that you are being unfair in this situation." "I really want to communicate with you without using profanity." I know this is not a real option in prison, but if you are on parole or probation, this is something that is important for you to grasp as it impacts your continued freedom.

Einstein's definition of insanity is doing the same thing over and over while expecting a different result.

You will have to speak to people every day in the free world. You will have to interact with others to survive, and if you want to thrive, interaction is mandatory. Humans are social creatures, and social interaction is a necessary part of life. You will speak thousands of words each day, so do not just throw them out of your mouth. Never take for granted that others will automatically understand how you feel or what you want. Never take communication with others lightly. And remember that words once spoken can rarely be taken back.

The past is dead; you are not your past. The future has not yet happened. You have only the present moment, from moment to moment, and your choices within each moment will become your future. Seeing this process can begin growth in a new direction.

Your tone of voice, facial expressions, body language, and your sentence construction are all under your control. YOUR COMPLETE CONTROL ALWAYS. No excuses. Once words come out of your mouth, you cannot retrieve them. Do not use words as weapons or camouflage because that way of communication will lead you back into chaos with people in general and society always. You must communicate honestly and speak straight to people. Prison has crippled your ability to speak honestly and straightforwardly because, in many ways, this kind of healthy communication is not safe in prison. Remember that you are not in prison any longer, and you need to adapt to the environment you are in—the free world environment.

Your choices in the present moment become your future.

There are some excellent ways to improve your ability to speak straightforwardly and honestly.

1. Never use clichés or slang when you communicate with others, either in writing or verbally. The majority of people in society will think you have intelligence challenges or a dull mind. They will simply assume you cannot think for yourself, or they will see you as emotionally stunted and immature. Sayings like "Nobody talks, and everybody walks" or "Instant retaliation ensures no future violation" just ensure that you look less intelligent to free people. They will judge you as inferior, and they will treat you that way when it comes to job promotions, interviews, social situations, and general upward mobility. In

the free world, clichés, profanity, and slang are considered the tools of people who only have the lowest base level of intelligence. They are not the clever social skills they are perceived as within prison. People will assume you are crude, rude, and unintelligent. And you thought you were so "on point" doing it inside prison. You were always right, and everyone else was stupid, clueless, and always wrong. You were one superior cage-dwelling human. Let's move on from prison.

Your past is only an ancient reflection of old choices invalidated by new growth in the present moment.

2. Try your best to not use unnecessary interjections in your speech when talking to other people. Words like "Man," "You know," and "Uh," only frustrate people who are listening to you. If you use these interjections too often in your sentences, people will eventually tune you out and stop listening. There is no need to be angry over this phenomenon because it is just natural human behavior. People will not listen or give their attention to someone who makes it hard to do so. They will lose focus on what you are trying to communicate.

Your biggest challenge in the free world will lie in how you present yourself to others.

3. Try to avoid using words you are not comfortable using. You cannot hope to impress anyone with multisyllabic words you just learned yesterday. Strive to remain true to your own natural and personal speech patterns. Do not be "that person"—the person using complex words incorrectly, oblivious that they are doing so.

Choices are everywhere, and choices impact the future as well as the present.

4. Avoid profanity. Inside prison, profanity quickly becomes "normal" language. Profanity is sprinkled throughout everyday conversation. Within the confines of the prison world, profanity is rampant and immune to every rule of grammar. Profane words are not just adjectives, they cross all lines and become nouns, verbs, personal pronouns—they become part of almost all syntax. Profane communication becomes the norm and experiences no barriers within prison walls.

Profanity is almost always a challenge for someone reentering society after prison. Eliminating profanity from your daily speech is well worth the effort when you realize the price of profanity in the free world. One slip can cost you a job offer, a relationship, a chance at something new. You will be judged by your speech. It's best to accept this fact, or you can lose societal credibility. It is your choice. *Einstein's definition of insanity is doing the same thing over and over while expecting a different result.*

For many former inmates, profanity presents a particularly difficult challenge simply because profanity has become part of their internal dialog. Your biological computer oversees your speech because you have created the connections for it to do so. You will have to create non-profane connections within your biological computer. Luckily, connections that are not used grow weak, and connections that are used frequently grow strong. You will have to take control and build new connections within your biological computer that support and sustain your new growth in a healthier direction. You must resist and tame the profane urge. There was a time in your life when you did not speak that way. You can make that happen again with some effort. In the free world, people will judge you by your speech and the content of your language. They will also judge the content of your character by your speech as well.

Choices are everywhere, and choices impact the future as well as the present. Allowing your ego to rule your choices will lead only to despair. Everyone else will be wrong, and you will always be right. You will win every battle and lose the ultimate war for your freedom. Even when you are free of the criminal justice system, you will still be an inmate. You will think like an inmate and act like an inmate. You will eventually return to the place where inmates live out their lives. All of it will reflect your choices.

You can be upset about the role language plays in the social world. You can whine, play victim, argue about "freedom of speech," and resist the truth. The Supreme Court has upheld hate speech as protected speech. That is how much we, as a society, admire and value freedom of speech. However legal and protected, profanity and hate speech will neither get you a job nor sustain a career. Like it or not, the words you choose to use will have social and personal consequences. Profanity will not open doors for you, and it can crush your dreams. Words are powerful. Use them wisely and with discretion.

Your choices in the present moment become your future.

5. Try to avoid talking down to people. On the same note, try to avoid talking up to people, too. In a free society, both practices are regarded as signs of insecurity. In a free society, people who stand for nothing are weak, and the common view is that anything will knock them over. Alternately, while it is important to have an opinion, those who try to force their opinion on others who may not agree are seen as negative, pushy, unintelligent, and insecure. Whenever you can, practice speaking in a simple, straightforward manner. Use as few words as possible to communicate your position. Try to create sentences that are concise, yet information-packed.

Read the novel *The Old Man and the Sea* by Ernest Hemingway for sentence construction examples. Pay attention to how he constructs some of his sentences. They tend to be short, concise, and information-packed sentences. Simple sentences carrying complex thoughts are respected. They do not waste time, and they pack in a lot of information. Uncluttered language, free of profanity, is powerful. People tend to listen to this kind of communication because it keeps their attention. Do not clutter your language and communication with rude adjectives or needless figures of speech. Pay attention to your body language, facial expression, and tone of voice as you speak. Speaking well to others is a powerful skill. Learn to use this effectively.

If possible, record yourself speaking on video. Then play it back and listen closely to your communication skills. A video recording can be brutal in its detached honesty. This will help you correct the most blatant errors in your speech. Often, a person has no idea how they present themselves to the world, so watching yourself speak can be a great help in becoming a good, effective communicator.

When you meet new people, you will have only that present moment in time to present yourself. Your choices in language, speech, body language, tone of voice, and facial expression will convey an image. That image will be interpreted as "you" by the new people meeting you for the first time. Choose wisely when you present yourself (your SELF) to the world. You have only the present moment, so use that precious moment in time well.

Living within the free world, within a society made up of people who only know freedom, can be challenging to former prisoners. This is because prisoners come out of prison with expectations. Society does not agree with most of the expectations that prisoners hold. Society, in general, does not feel that prisoners are owed jobs, housing, medical care, food, clothing, or even a second chance. Society generally thinks that prisoners need to prove themselves first in order to gain opportunities.

Society generally feels that prisoners need them, and that society does not need prisoners. If you hope to remain free within a free society, you will have to know the rules and play by those rules. In a free society, you will be exposed to an incredibly complex barrage of people, obligations, responsibilities, and events. How capable you are of dealing with this onslaught will directly affect your survival on parole.

Your prison mentality has taught you to play the victim and think you can demand things from life—that you are automatically entitled to things. Free people know that life demands things from us, and we are entitled to nothing except what we earn. Strength to free people is the ability to respond well to life's demands. The entitlement mentality, the victim mentality—these are weaknesses. Society admires people who lead creative, organized lives and people who are efficient and responsible with their resources. You must believe that you can become this kind of person if you want to survive parole and stay free.

Chapter Five Personal Development Questions

Use a separate sheet of paper for these exercises.

In a medical dictionary, look up the following words and write out the definitions:

> *Frontal Lobe*
> *Corpus Callosum*
> *Right Hemisphere*
> *Left Hemisphere*
> *Limbic System*
> *Amygdala*
> *Hypothalamus*

Using a regular dictionary, look up the following words and write the definitions:

> *Entitlement*
> *Victim*
> *Cliché*
> *Slang*
> *Strength*
> *Threat*
> *Society*

Chapter Five Essay Questions

Write five paragraphs on why honesty is important within society and how it helps the individual and society overall.

Write out ten reasons why you like yourself.

Write out four things you would like to change about yourself and why you want to make these changes. Be specific. How will these changes serve your new growth and how will they add to the betterment of yourself and society? Feel free to use extra sheets of paper or write this out in your personal journal.

Name five things you would like to accomplish within the next five years. Include how each of these goals will improve you as a person and better your position within society.

Chapter Five Book Recommendation

Read *The Old Man and the Sea* by Earnest Hemmingway. This book is in addition to the reading list at the end of this book. Write out some of your thoughts and impressions.

Chapter Five Affirmation

1. *I am my true self and I effortlessly communicate with others the truth of my being.*

CHAPTER SIX

Becoming Employed

You are required to have a job while you are on parole or probation. But if you think about it, you must find meaningful and fulfilling work if you want to be happy and content within society anyway. This is true even if you were never in prison or on parole or probation. Becoming employed and entering the taxpayer ranks is one of the biggest challenges that many ex-prisoners and addicts face when reentering society. Failure to obtain and maintain a job will eventually lead to you violating the conditions of your release and getting sent back to jail or prison. Having a job is a powerful catalyst that will help you stay free. A job will help you survive parole or probation. Thus, it is of primary importance.

WORK IS A SURVIVAL TACTIC

A job is one of the best and strongest tools in your survival tool chest. Humans are social creatures and interacting at work with other humans can be rewarding and fun. All workplaces have a unique culture and becoming part of that culture—having meaningful work—gives you a sense of purpose. Of course, many people who work together become friends and socialize, too. This makes sense when you realize that shared work and workplace experiences always help people create, build, and cement strong bonds.

Consider the positive possibilities.

For a three-year parole or probation obligation, you will have to survive 1,095 days. It will serve your best survival interest if you can do that with no negative law enforcement contact, and only positive interactions with your parole/probation officer. As a matter of fact, positive interactions with your PO and no negative law enforcement contacts are a perfect recipe for success and long-term freedom. It can be done, and there is no reason why you cannot achieve this. One thousand ninety-five days are a lot of days; remember that you are not free yet. You are a prisoner on a short leash, and you are being tested. You are a prisoner on parole—do not ignore that fact. You must earn your freedom, and while you do just that, remember to fill up your self-esteem tank. (Set goals and accomplish them.)

(The past is dead; you are not your past. The future has not yet happened. You have only the present moment, from moment to moment, and your choices in each moment will become your future. Seeing this process can begin growth in a new direction.)

A job takes up a lot of time, and it also provides a solid record of your whereabouts each day or night depending upon your work schedule. Work is truly a survival tactic. One of your biggest threats will be old so-called "friends" and "associates." Many will still be "in the game," meaning that they will be in their thirties or forties, perpetual felons, emotionally immature, codependent, self-centered, ego-ruled, drug-using people with serious criminal and addictive-thinking errors. They will always be right, everyone else will always be wrong, and they will be on law enforcement's radar. If you become weak and decide to run with them occasionally for "old times' sake," you will eventually end up in a cage.

You will be embracing old patterns, old choices, and a past lifestyle that cannot lead you to your true purpose or long-term happiness.

Choices are everywhere, and choices impact the future as well as the present. Allowing your ego to rule your choices will lead only to despair. Everyone else will be wrong, and you will always be right. You will win every battle and lose the ultimate war for your freedom. Even when you are free of the criminal justice system, you will be an inmate. You will think like an inmate and act like an inmate. You will eventually return to the place where inmates live out their lives. All of it will reflect your choices.

You will feel conflicted about old "friends." If you examine the toxic dynamic, you will clearly see that these "friendships" were really all about narcissistic abuse, codependency, drug use, and the criminal lifestyle. The interactions were based on nonstop thinking errors and self-centered, ego-driven motives that are rooted in the culture of addiction and criminality. These "friends" were always right, and everyone else was always wrong—even you. They will always pressure you into their way of thinking. So think about this for a minute: Why do they need you in the mix? If the car is pulled over and drugs are found, you will be the one going back to jail. These "friends" will expect you to obey the convict code of "Nobody talks, and everyone walks," but this is unequivocally not true.

Your participation only benefits their self-centered, ego-driven, twisted worldview. The guy on probation takes the fall—always—and you will do the time for your "friend's" dope. How convenient for your "friends." If you fight it and refuse to take the fall, you are a "snitch," and it's now "go time" with your "friends." There is nothing noble about emotionally stunted, selfish, forever adolescent, perpetual felons. They consistently make stupid decisions. Interacting with them only leads to chaos, drama, incarceration, and a life diverted from its true purpose.

A survivor does not expect others to make his survival choices. Why would you allow ego-driven, narcissistic, immature people who are living the criminal and addictive lifestyle to make your survival decisions? If they cared about you at all, they would encourage your new growth and never want to place you in harm's way. These old "friends" will endanger your freedom and eventually crush your dreams. They need you because they don't want to get flushed down society's toilet alone. They want some company in the cesspool when they arrive. They want to know people once they get back to their comfort zone, prison. They want someone to share lies with as they live in denial and allow their ego to run amok, doing life on the installment plan once again. You are not your past choices, but you will become your present choices.

A job can help you distance yourself from old "friends" and outdated habits that are invalidated by your new growth. When approached by old friends and associates, you can always blame your parole officer or your boss for a heavy workload. Think like a survivor. If they run into you randomly, simply say you are on your way to meet your parole officer for a meeting. If possible, I recommend that you work overtime for the entire duration of your probation or parole. Work two jobs if you can. These proactive actions on your part will take a huge chunk out of the 1,095 days you must survive. Being proactive will help you live through supervision without drama and violations.

Choices are everywhere, and choices impact the future as much as the present.

You can use the world of work as well as your parole officer to shield you from these outdated challenges to your freedom and survival. Tell your parole agent what you are doing for work. If every time your parole agent checks on you, he finds you at work or home recovering from work, you will eventually become boring. Boring is GOOD when you are on parole/probation. A typical parole officer has a huge caseload, and they may have many "squeaky wheels" that need additional grease. If you prove over time that you are not ever in need of that extra grease, your parole officer will focus on more exciting clients. After all, there are only twenty-four hours in a day. You must eat, sleep, work, take care of household chores, and pay bills. The more you fill these hours with work and positive endeavors, the safer you are on parole or probation. Become that boring person to your parole officer. You simply will not have a lot of time available to become drawn into negative situations and drama surrounding old "friends." As they say in prison, "Make time serve you; stop serving time." If you want to change other people's opinions, show them rather than tell them. To be an example requires choice always."

Your choices within the present moment become your future. Your parole officer will always know where you are and what you are up to when you make work a survival tactic. Your former "friends" still living that old lifestyle will move on to other victims and play their dysfunctional games with them instead of you. Eventually, your old associates will end up in prison again because they are committed to serving life on the installment plan. Some will die of Hepatitis C and others of HIV. Some will overdose. Some will die due to violence. Their lifestyle choices will take them away from you eventually. Since your old "friends" are still thinking like inmates while out in the free world, they are destined to return to the place where inmates live out their lives—prison. Thinking and choices create situations around you, and these situations impact your life for the better or the worse.

When you were in prison, you were forced to work for free or for penny wages. If you were lucky enough to even obtain one of the soul-crushing, sometimes nasty jobs at least it relieved your overwhelming boredom for a time. Even if you must take a minimum wage job at first, just know it is a beginning and not an end. You are starting over again. You have the power to choose your attitude about the situation. Always remember that you are still an inmate. You are an inmate on parole or probation. No one owes you anything, and you are not entitled to anything. Society and life, in general, are putting demands on you, and you are in no position to demand anything from life. Now is your time to deliver and prove yourself. In doing so, you will create a new, more positive existence for yourself. You have a much larger pay grade than you had in prison. Remember also that you will improve, and this first survival job is not your final destination.

Your prison mentality has taught you to simultaneously play both victim and predator and to think that you can demand things from life. That you are automatically entitled to things. Free people know that life demands things from us, and we are entitled to nothing except what we earn. Strength, to free people, is the ability to respond well to all these life demands. The entitlement mentality, the victim mentality, the predator mentality—these are symptoms of an unbalanced life, and society perceives these traits as true weakness. Society admires people who lead creative, organized lives. People who are efficient and responsible with their resources. You must believe that you can become this kind of person if you want to survive parole and stay free.

I knew a probationer who could not find a job due to his felony. Finally, he was hired for counter work at a cookie store. He was ashamed and angry with the world that this was the only job he could get after a drug conviction. He had a college degree, and he was a veteran. How dare society "do this to him." He believed the judge was unfair. That society was unfair. That his probation officer was unfair. He hated his life and what it had become. He wanted to go back to drug dealing and his past lifestyle because the money was better. He hated the world. He "deserved" better than this.

Allowing your ego to rule your choices will lead only to despair.

We talked about it, and I helped him see some positive possibilities. We were both veterans, and I shared with him the idea that, as veterans, we knew that sometimes life demands things from us and that we cannot always dictate what comes our way. We processed the fact that we can only control our actions when life delivers demands, we cannot control the actions of others. I reminded him of the radical acceptance that a soldier must sometimes embrace not out of free choice but out of necessity. I pointed out that the cookie store was a national chain and that they had hired him with full knowledge that he was an ex-felon. They believed in him and offered him a chance to prove himself. They were not dwelling on his past, so why was he? They were not offering a punishment, only an open and honest chance to make different choices. They were offering him an opportunity within the present moment, and they were indifferent to his past. Why was he using his precious present moment to dwell on the past and on people who have nothing to do with this present moment? Why was he allowing the past to rent space in his mind and impact a present opportunity?

He quickly worked his way up to assistant manager and then manager of one store while also accepting responsibility as an assistant manager of another. He did this while on probation. He is now off probation and manages two stores for the chain, with one of them being located within a prestigious high-traffic area in a major metropolitan city. The other is in a trendy boutique area in the same city. With sales bonuses, he makes close to one hundred thousand dollars a year. That is more than he ever made dealing drugs, and the retirement and medical plan are a lot better. He is off parole and married to a beautiful, intelligent nurse. Together, he and his wife have a beautiful child and a fine home. Not bad for a guy who started out behind the cookie counter fresh out of jail making minimum wage.

"Simple joys are the most lasting."

By seeing his first job out of prison as an opportunity rather than a punishment or a chore, he rose quickly. He was made assistant manager in a year. By year two, he was managing one store and assistant managing another. By year three, he was off probation early and managing both stores. He never saw his old "associates" again because they all went back to prison. He moved on. He never wanted to sell cookies, but life demanded something of him. When he surrendered to the demands of life and practiced acceptance rather than serving his ego, he found success. When he found purpose and learned the value of service to others he found a success that he had never thought possible, and a new life he had never been able to envision before prison.

Since he began practicing acceptance and seeing his life as one of service, he has grown in many ways. He has given many others new chances just as he was once given a chance. And the universe has blessed him for he has been a catalyst for growth to others. He is in a wonderful relationship with a supportive partner, has gained a new respect for himself, and has been blessed with having his felony dismissed. All rights and privileges have been restored to him through expungement. He does not judge others for their past, just as a kind person once did for him. When he felt worthless, someone saw his potential. Now, he passes this gift on to others, quietly and humbly, just as it was given to him.

> "Lord, grant that I might not so much seek to be loved as to love."
> —St. Francis of Assisi

At one time, this client of mine had felt hopeless and alienated from society. He could only envision himself dealing drugs again for a living. He saw himself as a victim and possessed virtually no self-esteem. He eventually built self-esteem the old-fashioned way—he saw his opportunity as a beginning rather than an end, as a blessing rather than a punishment. He set goals, and he accomplished them. By embracing acceptance and walking behind that cookie counter, he put himself on a path to happiness yet unknown to him.

Free people know that life demands things from us, and we are entitled to nothing except what we earn through our own honest effort.

Parole or probation can be a tough beginning, but it is just that—a beginning. It is not the end. Neither is your first job. You never know where a positive attitude will lead you because no one knows the future. Just know with all certainty that your choices in the present moment are shaping your future, even though it is a future you cannot see until it becomes your present moment down the road. Travel your road with a positive attitude, with acceptance, with a sense of service to others, and with wise choices. Your choices will determine your life.

Your past is an ancient reflection of old choices that have been invalidated by new growth in the present moment. Choose wisely.

Parole and probation officers are humans, too. Resenting them for their role in your life is an exercise in futility. Resentment is useless. This dysfunctional thinking cannot serve your higher good. Remember that resentment and its co-occurring anger are secondary emotions. You are most likely angry at a cluster of resentments due to your own past choices. Choices that led you to the incarceration process in general, and the criminal justice system in particular, (which can be less than warm and fuzzy.) The parole officer represents the system to you, and you are not happy with the system. However, deep down, you are unhappy with yourself. You are unhappy with your choices and your life currently. I am telling you that it does not have to stay this way.

No one in the criminal justice system ever asked for you by name. You showed up and entered the system because of the choices you made. You entered their world by choice. They didn't enter your world; you drew them to you through your actions and your decisions. They had no choice but to meet you. They are just doing their job. You had the choice to avoid them entirely by choosing law-abiding behavior, but you chose the opposite. It is your fault that they are in your life. They never had the option of hanging up a No Vacancy sign.

You can choose how you deal with this situation. Working long hours, working two jobs or an extra part-time job, working and going to school—these are actions respected by a free society. It has been a tried-and-true method of success for centuries. My father did it to get through law school and pay the bills. A good friend did it for a down payment on a house. You can do it also. It is always your choice. It is in your best interest to cultivate being quiet, respectful, and above all, hardworking. Be the person your employer can rely on to be punctual—to come early—and to stay late to finish the job.

Consider the virtue of service to others. Service, in many ways, is much more satisfying than the monetary reward. Acceptance, service, and surrender are powerful forces that you can harness to propel your efforts in the workplace to levels that you did not know existed. Accept your situation. You are beginning again and becoming employed is a much-needed survival tool in your life. You are not free yet—you are a prisoner on parole. You have very few rights. Your parole officer and law enforcement have the ability and power to take back this freedom if they deem it necessary. Accept the reality of your current situation.

I would like you to again consider the meaning of the word "survival." Webster's New World Dictionary, Third College Edition, defines survival as: "the act, state, or fact of surviving." It goes on to define survival as "something or someone who survives." Researching a bit further in Webster's, we find the word "survive." The definition of this word that I like best is: "to continue to live after or in spite of." The example used in Webster's is: "to continue to live after, or in spite of, a shipwreck." If you are in prison, in jail, or on parole, your life is officially a "shipwreck." You are not sailing through life; you are crashing on the rocks of the criminal justice system, and no ship ever created can sail upon rocks and remain afloat.

Service to others is a truly wonderful thing. When you make one person smile you automatically smile with them. This is powerful because it reflects the best within our human existence. Finding true purpose in service is a beautiful road to freedom. This road can only lead away from prison—never towards prison. Service to others and finding purpose in performing such service is the only true freedom. You cannot see the future, but you can always see the path in front of you as you walk that path. Choosing service is choosing a new life.

Your choices in the present moment become your future. Your choices determine your life. Make time serve you and stop serving time.

Surrender is a misunderstood concept by many ex-prisoners. You are in the process of creating a new life by making different life choices. Surrender in the context of re-creation means to let go of an old way of being in the world. You are not "giving up" on life, you are surrendering old ways and choices that cannot serve your present positive situation. Far from being defeated, you are empowered when you let go of old, destructive habits, and choices invalidated by a need for new growth. Acceptance, service, and surrender are your new tools in your survival tool chest. Use them well, and they will serve you well.

Consider the positive possibilities.

I recommend that you be honest and upfront about your time in prison with potential employers. This will serve you well in the long run. I have interviewed too many prisoners who have lost their jobs due to lying on an employment application. Simply list the jobs you did in prison, the courses you completed, and be honest. If you shy away from this challenge, you will limit your job growth and advancement. Also, you will always be stressed out and worried that your employer may find out about your past. A visit to your workplace by your parole officer could put you in an uncomfortable situation. Being honest with an employer upfront prevents negativity and drama down the road.

Make time serve you and stop serving time.

I know an ex-prisoner who lied on his application for a utility company and was hired. He had a great job for about four years. Then he was promoted due to his great work. The problem was, once he was in management, he had to be bonded. The company found out about his prison time and checked his application. Even though he had been a great worker, the company policy was to terminate anyone who had lied on their application. He was terminated even though his boss did not want that outcome. It became a human resource matter and company policy was clear. They could not make an exception because the policy had to be fair across the board for everyone. Had he been honest, he could have been bonded through the felony bonding program, and all would have been upfront. You can find out about this program in the resources section of this workbook.

Your choices in the present moment become your future.

Everything is earned in the free world. Money, opportunities, respect, and credibility. Never lie on an application. It may take a little longer to get hired, but in the long run, it is a lot better for you and your life goals. It is far more positive to get a chance at a job and show your new employer what you can do, and what you are truly capable of accomplishing. Earning real respect is far better than stealing an opportunity through deceit or lying by omission. Having a criminal record is a challenge but never a problem. Challenges, as opposed to problems, can be met and dealt with.

A survival job is often a necessity as you train for a career. You can choose to work a survival job and train for a better career. Many people have followed this path and are better off for having done so. You can build a résumé while you train for an occupation where a felony record will not hold you back. If you must struggle for a while in a survival job, just remember that you are a work in progress. You are not a finished product—you're just starting to become who you want to be.

It is not the end. It is a new beginning—a new journey. Start this journey honestly.

Take the time you need for training. Working and training is the time when you learn new skills, meet new people, learn new ways of thinking about things, network, and learn a new way of being in the world. You are not worthless; you are a human being, and there is a purpose that you need to find and fulfill. Searching for that purpose is a rewarding path to lifelong freedom and happiness. You are not condemned to low-paying jobs for the rest of your life. No matter your age or your current position, you can still make goals and have higher-purpose aspirations. It is up to you alone to identify, choose, and pursue those goals.

We are entitled to nothing except what we earn.

There are six cold, hard facts about ex-prisoners that I will share with you now:

1. To make it in society and gain respect, ex-felons must be above reproach.
2. Ex-felons must be more talented than the competition in their chosen field because they will always be judged harsher.
3. Ex-felons will never be trusted completely by most people who learn of their past.

4. Ex-felons must become more honorable, honest, and respectable than the average person because society will always judge an ex-felon harsher. Don't believe me? Look at how sentencing laws are applied as an example. No matter how many years have passed, how does law enforcement treat you at a traffic stop?
5. You must work smarter and harder than others to obtain what you need.
6. You must change from within using acceptance, forgiveness, and surrender.

When you meet people who judge you by your past, just know they are living in the past. Refuse to argue with them. Do not try to convince them of anything. It is a waste of time. They are speaking from their ego and the ego just wants to make everyone wrong and itself right—always. They are trying to bring up your past to make you "wrong" in the present. You are not your past. When you become defensive or argue with them, you are just playing ego games. You are doubting yourself and your present moment choices. You are giving away your personal power by accepting their negativity. You are living in the past right alongside them. You are losing time in the present, and your energy is focused on defending your ego rather than your new growth and new path. You are squandering your energy on the past.

Far from being defeated, you are empowered when you let go of old, destructive habits and choices invalidated by the need for new growth. Acceptance, service, and surrender are your new tools in your survival tool chest. Use them well, and they will serve you well.

Since first impressions are forever, show up to job interviews prepared and on time. Bring extra copies of transcripts, letters of recommendation, your résumé, and any job-related certificates you have earned. Allow the interviewer to control the flow and pace of the interview. This may be hard for you to do after years in prison but do it anyway. Do not exaggerate, brag, and never volunteer information about your past that is not specifically asked for by the interviewer. Do not speak ill of former employers, coworkers, or the prison system. Never smoke or ask for a smoke break. And stay off your cell phone.

You have only the present moment, from moment to moment, and your choices in each moment will become your future.

Dress modestly and neatly. Do not show up to a job interview with sagging pants that show off your butt cheeks and boxers with a sideways baseball cap on your head. Unless you hate work, of course. Cover up any tattoos that display nudity, mayhem, prison themes, or racial hatred. Do not wear shorts that display calf tattoos. Even if it is hot, wear long pants. Try to research the company online so you can go to the interview prepared with some knowledge about the company's mission statement and goals. Make sure you can speak about their products and services. If the interviewer asks you what you know about the company, you will be able to converse with some confidence on the topic. Also, try to visit the company site in advance to get an idea about the dress code. If you do not have a computer, ask a friend for help, or go to the public library and use a computer there. Do not bring friends, and do not have anyone wait in the car for you during the interview process.

When you meet new people, you have only that present moment in time to make an impression. Your choice of language, speech, body language, tone of voice, and facial expressions will create an image of you. That image will be interpreted as "you" by the new people meeting you for the first time. Choose wisely when you present yourself (your SELF) to the world. You have only the present moment, so use that precious moment in time well.

Remember to be honest, but also remember that it is OK to minimize past challenges whenever possible. You cannot expect free people to understand your past challenges in prison or your old criminal lifestyle. Instead of saying that you were a drug dealer for the Mexican Mafia, you could share that you once had a substance abuse challenge, but you are now in recovery. Never make things sound worse than they really are.

If the interviewer asks about your past, let them know that you are a good person today and your challenges are in your past. Let them know about current life, training, hobbies, and healthy pastimes. Always bring the conversation back to the present moment whenever possible. Make sure your handshake is warm, firm, and dry. Ask for the interviewer's business card after the job interview. Write them a thank you card and mail it that evening so that they remember you. Even if you are not hired now, they may hire you later because they remember you in a positive light.

You have only the present moment, so use that precious moment in time well.

I have one more tip about interviews. Bring along a fact sheet to every interview. Have a few copies ready to hand out to the interviewer if needed. A fact sheet is not a résumé. A fact sheet has your personal information and references, whereas a résumé never has references included. A fact sheet has your driver's license number, military information, dates of employment, skills, education information, and most importantly, references. You can refer to your fact sheet during the interview process, and if references are requested, you have them readily available. A fact sheet also demonstrates how well you have prepared for this interview with the potential employer. Employers tend to notice and like well-prepared applicants.

Make time serve you and stop serving time.

Remember that your goal is not just to survive but to eventually thrive. Living well is fun. Work and school are survival situations for everyone—not just ex-prisoners. I am still taking work-related courses in counseling and case management after almost twenty years in the field. Learning never stops in the modern workforce. People are always updating skills, and learning is a lifelong process. You can survive anything with enough hope and desire. You survived prison because you had a release date, and you associated hope with a better life after that date. You have an end date for probation or parole as well. Until that discharge date, I recommend that you fill your days with work, training, or both. Your continued freedom depends upon it. Your future quality of life surely does also.

Earning real respect is far better than tricking your way into an opportunity. Having a criminal record is a challenge but never a problem. Remember that challenges can be met and dealt with. Far from being defeated, you are most empowered when you let go of old, destructive habits and choices invalidated by the need for new growth. Acceptance, service, and surrender are your new tools in your survival tool chest. Use them well, and they will serve you well.

JOB HUNTING IS A JOB

Make your job hunt a forty-hour-per-week, full-time job. Most parolees put in a few applications, visit a state employment development office, and then wait around to see what happens. Do not be that person because work is a survival tactic. Blanket your city with hundreds of applications. Parole agents tend to respect people who try hard to do the right thing. Most state employment development departments have job centers where you can get help with cover letters, résumé writing, job boards, and training. Some of these resources may also be online. Most of these state-run job centers have a veteran's specialist and a felony job specialist on-site to assist you with your job search.

Temp agencies are also a good starting point. Many temp agencies place ex-felons in a variety of positions. Employers like temp agencies because they have a chance to see how you work out without a lengthy interview and hiring process. Many temp jobs can lead to permanent placement with an employer. Since the employer saves money, and they trust the temp agency to screen you, you benefit because you may get a chance to prove yourself to a company. A company that may not have considered you during their standard hiring process. I have seen this happen with a client I worked with. She built up such a good reputation with her work ethic that she was offered a job with a Fortune 500 company and is now on her way to a six-figure income.

SIGN HUNTING

Sign hunting is a technique used successfully by many newly released ex-prisoners. Eighty percent of all jobs are not advertised because businesses hang help wanted signs or use temp agencies. Sign hunting can help you get an interview right on the spot just for inquiring about a job. The benefit to you is that you can often be seen by the person doing the hiring. Sign hunting simply means that you canvass your community and local industrial parks for help wanted signs, fill out applications, and hopefully meet people along the way. Make sure to bring your fact sheet with you and have a lot of copies ready. Résumés are premeeting screening tools. This means that most newly released ex-felons have a harder time getting a chance to meet employers face-to-face. Especially when they only have prison jobs to report. Sign hunting can get you started in the employment world.

NETWORKING

Do not hesitate to use Narcotics Anonymous (NA) and Alcoholics Anonymous (AA) contacts for job opportunities. Let people know at meetings that you have employment challenges. You must learn to ask for help when you need it. If you attend religious services, let the pastor, rabbi, priest, or imam know that you are seeking employment. Let them know about the challenges you face as an ex-felon. Also, do not forget about your local public library and college job boards. Both places have resources you can use to find work. Libraries also have the latest local newspapers to browse and computers to use for your online applications.

Do not forget local union halls when considering opportunities for work. A parolee from Pelican Bay in his early fifties started out as a laborer in the Ironworkers Union. Within two years, he was a union welder. Good things happen when you refuse to give up and decide to make things happen.

Make time serve you and stop serving time.

RÉSUMÉ

A résumé is a screening tool, and as I pointed out earlier, it can be a blessing or a curse. If you have been locked up for many years and have gained few vocational or educational skills while in prison, a résumé will most likely screen you out of the majority of jobs. I recommend that you use sign hunting, networking, temp agencies, and the local state job center to resolve your employment challenges. Remember that most of the time, you create your own luck. If you have some vocational training and any past employment history, then I recommend that you use the local job center for a résumé workshop. These classes are ongoing. You will get help with writing cover letters, creating copies of your documents, and most importantly, updating your current résumé and cover letter to adhere to the most up-to-date formats that employers are seeking. Employers regularly throw away résumés that are in an outdated style or on the wrong kind of paper. The cover letter format seems to change with résumé styles every few years. Your best strategy is to use the formats that the local employment development department recommends in your state.

TOOLS

The following items will make your work and personal life much easier. These are not just tools for parole but tools for life. Almost everyone in the free world uses these tools regularly.

1. A watch. It does not have to be a luxury timepiece—it just needs to accurately keep the time.
2. A small notebook for addresses and phone numbers as a backup to your cell phone.
3. A pen for your notebook and life in general.
4. A calendar. One for home and one for work. Make sure it has room for you to write all over it.
5. A cell phone. You need one for communication as pay phones are almost non-existent. If you have been locked down for a while, this may be a shock. There are mobile apps available for every one of the aforementioned tools, but you should always have a backup. Always have a car charger and a regular wall charger for your phone.
6. A laptop or notebook computer. If you do not have one, get one now. Learn to use it well. The world is fast, and you will have to keep up. Classes are offered in some stores and most computers come with built-in tutorials, so you can literally "plug in and go."

Once you develop the habit of using your notebook and calendars, your life will be more organized and simpler to manage. Your calendar is the place for you to keep track of all work and social obligations. Birthdays, holidays, meetings with your parole officer, and your work schedule should all be noted consistently on your calendar. Always remember to back up all your data on your electronic devices and keep a copy of important phone numbers in your paper notebook.

Make time serve you and stop serving time.

Make sure you use that watch and be punctual. People will judge you in the free world by how you use and manage time. Writing things down and accomplishing tasks will benefit you in many ways. You will accomplish more, feel better, feel more in control of your life, gain self-esteem, and be more satisfied with yourself, your goals, and your overall life.

MEETINGS WITH YOUR PAROLE OFFICER

Record on paper and electronically all meetings with your parole officer. Every date and time, what you discussed, your obligations met and unmet. Keep all copies of fines and restitution you have paid, including dates and times. If your parole officer gives you instructions, record the dates and times you carried out those instructions. Record the dates and times of all urine tests and the results. Record your compliance with all registration requirements that you have been ordered to comply with.

It is not the end. It is a new beginning, a new journey. Start this journey honestly.

Do not use the top of your refrigerator or TV as a filing cabinet. If you do not have a filing cabinet, buy one and use it. Buy some file folders and a cardboard box if that is all you can afford at first. Begin to keep records now. You are learning to live as a free person, and this takes some effort and planning on your part. Sitting on the couch eating chips will not do it for you. Other people will not do it for you. Living free and legal is a journey. It will require some time and energy on your part. You will not have time for old, outdated, negative thinking errors or criminal thinking. Your old way of life will become invalidated by the new growth inherent within meeting the challenges of free life.

Far from being defeated, you are empowered when you let go of old, destructive habits and choices that have become invalidated by your new need for growth. Acceptance, service, and surrender are your new tools in your survival tool chest. Use them well, and they will serve you well. Your choices in the present moment will become your future.

Chapter Six Exercises

1. *Look up three temporary employment agencies in your area.*

If you are incarcerated currently, send each agency a letter and request information about their services. Be sure to enclose a stamped, self-addressed envelope so you can receive a response. If you are currently on probation or parole, email each agency and inquire about their services. Follow up with a phone call and make an appointment to meet with someone from the agency.

2. *Look up the address of your local employment development department.*

If you are incarcerated currently, write to the employment office, and ask about their services for job seekers. Make sure to request information on seminars and specific services that pertain to felons. If you are on parole or probation, call the office and make an appointment to learn about their services and opportunities.

3. Look up the following words and write out the definitions.

   Image

   Work

   Need

   Want

Free people know that life demands things from us, and we are entitled to nothing except what we earn. Your past is only an ancient reflection of old choices invalidated by new growth. Your future is being created by your new choices within the present moment. Choose wisely.

Chapter Six Personal Development Questions

1. Describe your work ethic in three paragraphs.
2. Describe your ideal career.
3. What does the phrase "Doing what you love, loving what you do" mean to you?
4. Describe in four paragraphs or more the worst job you had in prison. Include why it was unpleasant and how you coped with doing it. Are these coping skills you learned on that job applicable in the free world? How are they applicable? How are they not applicable?

Good things happen when you refuse to give up and decide to make things happen.

Chapter Six Affirmation

1. *I am created from universal abundance thus I am universal abundance. I effortlessly attract opportunities to serve others in all I do.*

CHAPTER SEVEN

Look Truthfully at Your Life

Are you happy? Only you can make yourself happy. You may be happy when other people are in your life, but they cannot make you happy. True inner happiness comes from living an inspired life. What inspires you? Are you following that inspiration? I ask these questions because I want you to begin to consider these questions. There is one defining characteristic common to all the billions of humans living on planet earth. We all seek happiness in one form or another. Your past drug use and criminal lifestyle was, at its core, concerned with finding happiness. More money, more attractive partners, more fun, more of everything—period.

Happiness is a universal need, yet the true nature of happiness eludes most people, not just people in prison or on parole. The true nature of happiness is always singular. The fact that you are a unique individual guarantees that your personal definition of happiness will be different from someone else's definition. It is your job to find happiness for yourself. No one else can do that for you. No matter how wonderful or helpful another human being is to you, no matter how wonderful your external world is at this time, your own happiness can only be found within yourself.

KEEP AND MAINTAIN A JOURNAL

Write in your journal every day. It is OK if you miss a day due to work, life, or family. Write tomorrow. Keeping a journal helps you get to know yourself better. By "yourself," I mean your true, authentic self. Not the self you present in prison or to your parole officer. Your real self. To make and maintain positive change and gain your own internal happiness, you must meet four challenges. A journal will help you do this. These challenges are:

1. You must become your own best and closest friend.
2. You must make peace with your past the best you can.
3. You must know, understand, and accept your life right up to this point.
4. You must practice being in the moment because the present moment is all you have.

The past is dead; you are not your past. The future has not yet happened. You have only the present moment, from moment to moment. Your choices within each moment will become your future. Seeing this process can begin growth in a new direction.

Have you ever talked yourself out of a raise? Have you ever cut classes or just not studied because you just "knew" you would not pass the test? Have you ever met an attractive person you wanted to ask out, and then lost your nerve? Have there been jobs you were interested in, yet you never applied for out of fear of being rejected? Have you failed to speak up for yourself due to frustration or the rationalization that nobody understands you anyway?

How do you transform yourself, that person in the mirror, into your closest friend? You acknowledge yourself, accept your struggle, and surrender your old ways that no longer serve your best interests or foster new growth. You achieve freedom from your own past personal history. Your new personal history is being written right now as you read this workbook. Every present moment, from moment to moment, the choices, and thoughts within those countless present moments—they are creating your future and writing your history simultaneously. You do not have to allow the ghosts of past choices to haunt you forever. New choices will run them off for good eventually.

When you journal, look at past choices and explore options you did not know you had at the time. Journal what you would do differently if you could do it all over. Journal about how you have changed your outlook. Journal about challenges within your present moment. Journal your new life history one sentence at a time, one paragraph at a time. Your journal will become a map of your personal growth and progress. Your journal will become a way to look back at where (and who) you have been in the past. Read your journal with acceptance and surrender. Do this and you will find a way to move forward with courage, hope, and gratitude within the present moment.

The past is dead; you are not your past. The future has not yet happened. You have only the present moment, from moment to moment. Your choices within each moment will become your future. Seeing this process can begin growth in a new direction. Consider the positive possibilities. You had freedom from choice in prison, you have freedom of choice now. What will you do?

Seek out new experiences and journal these experiences. Try new foods, listen to different music, meet new people, learn a new sport, join a computer club or an archery club. Learn a martial art. Journal it all. The more you explore and practice making new choices, the better your life will become in the long run. The more you create chances for finding a passion, a driving force in your life that becomes your purpose. Once you begin living with purpose, you will be immersed in happiness. You will be thriving, not just surviving. Your old, self-destructive way of life will be a distant memory. Your new, purpose-driven life will consume you, and you will have found fulfillment.

Chapter Seven Exercises

Write out and describe in detail what the concept of purpose means to you.

1. *Write one page on resentment and how it hurts you socially.*
2. *Write a page on the last time you lost your temper and how it affected your life.*

Remember: Free people know that life demands things from us, and we are entitled to nothing except what we earn. Your past is only an ancient reflection of old choices invalidated by new growth and new choices within the present moment. Choose wisely.

The past is dead; you are not your past. The future has not yet happened. You have only the present moment, from moment to moment. Your choices within each moment will become your future. Seeing this process can begin growth in a new direction. Consider the positive possibilities. You had freedom from choice in prison, you have freedom of choice now. What will you do?

Far from being defeated, you are empowered when you surrender and let go of old, destructive habits and choices invalidated by the need for new growth. Acceptance, service, and surrender are your new tools in your survival tool chest. Use them well, and they will serve you well. Your choices within the present moment become your future. A survivor does not expect others to make his survival choices.

Allowing your ego to rule your choices leads only to despair. Everyone else will be wrong, and you will always be right. You will win every battle, but you will lose the ultimate war for your freedom. Even when you are free of the criminal justice system, you will be an inmate. You will think like an inmate and act like an inmate. You will eventually return to the place where inmates live out their lives. All of it will reflect your choices.

If you really knew how to survive in society, what were you doing in prison or jail? You are not your anger. Your past is only an ancient reflection of old choices invalidated by new growth in the present moment. You are not your past. You are who you choose to become. Your response is all yours—always. You cannot control what others do and say but you have total control over what you do and say. Consider the positive possibilities.

When you meet people who judge you by your past, just know that they are living in the past. Refuse to argue with them. Do not try to convince them of anything. It is a waste of time. They are speaking from their ego, and the ego just wants to make everyone wrong and itself right—always. They are trying to bring up your past to make you wrong in the present moment. You are not your past. When you become defensive or argue with them, you are just playing ego games. You are doubting yourself and your present moment choices. You are giving away your personal power by accepting their negativity, and you are living in the past right alongside them. You are losing time in the present, and your energy is focused on defending your own ego rather than your new growth, your new path. You are squandering your energy on the past. Always return to the present moment. Their judgment of your past is not your present. Leave them behind.

Chapter Seven Affirmation

1. *I am a Being-Becoming, no longer bound by my past, creating my perfect future within my present moment.*

CHAPTER EIGHT
Recommended Reading List and Resources

Recommended Reading List

Choose one book to read per month. Review the personal development questions in this workbook after you finish each book. If you are a fast reader and can read more than one book per month…Awesome!

1. *The Complete Idiot's Guide to Reinventing Yourself* by Jeff Davidson
2. *You Just Don't Understand* by Deborah Tannen, PhD
3. *7 Tools to Beat Addiction* by Stanton Peele, PhD
4. *The Manipulated Man* by Ester Vilar
5. *E Squared: Nine Do-It-Yourself Energy Experiments That Prove Your Thoughts Create Your Reality* by Pam Grout
6. *You Can Heal Your Life* by Louise Hay
7. *The Passionate Mind* by Joel Kramer
8. *A Theory of Everything* by Ken Wilber
9. *Grace and Grit* by Ken Wilber
10. *Art Heals: How Creativity Cures the Soul* by Shaun McNiff
11. *Tao Te Ching: An Illustrated Journey* by Lao Tzu (translated by Steven Mitchell)
12. *Ultimate Principles of Success and Wisdom* by Deepak Chopra

Resources

Good things happen when you refuse to give up and decide to make things happen.

Alcoholics Anonymous
AA World Services, P.O. Box 459 Grand Central Station, New York, NY 10163
Web: www.aa.org

Narcotics Anonymous
NA World Services, P.O. Box 9999, Van Nuys, CA 91409
Web: www.na.org
Call: 1-818-773-9999

The Salvation Army
Web: www.salvationarmy.org
For prison ministry and prisoner resources:
Salvation Army National Headquarters, 615 Slaters Lane P.O. Box 269, Alexandria, VA 22313
Web: http://www.salvationarmyusa.org/usa/prison-ministries

Catholic Charities
Catholic Charities, 2050 Ballenger Ave., Ste. 400, Alexandria, VA 22314
Call: (703)-549-1390
Web: www.catholiccharities.org

Felony Bonding Program
The McLaughlin Company, 9210 Corporate Blvd., Ste. 250, Rockville, MD 20850
Call: 1-800-233-2258 or 202-293-5566

The Federal Bonding Program provides fidelity bonding for the first six months of employment for individuals dealing with the negative effects of past convictions. If you are an ex-felon who needs bonding services as a job requirement, you should call the following toll-free number for the nearest location of the current workforce office or one-stop employment center near you, as well as the current telephone number of the state bonding coordinator for your state. In those states lacking a state bonding coordinator, all callers will be referred to the nearest career center or one-stop center for employment assistance.

Call: 1-877-US2-JOBS (1-877-872-5627)

The University of the People The University of the People is an online university dedicated to helping people gain education and training as a tuition-free, accredited online college. Check them out.

Web: www.uopeople.edu

Khan Academy Khan Academy is a nonprofit with the mission to provide free, world-class education for anyone, anywhere.

Web: www.khanacademy.org

> *"Just know that your choices in the present moment will shape your future. This is a sure and defining future you cannot see until it becomes your present moment down the road. Right now, you are choosing your traveling companions. You are choosing how you react to challenges and experiences. Travel your road with a positive attitude, acceptance, a sense of service to others, and wise choices. Your choices will determine your life. Choose wisely."*
> —Dante B. Kun